Excellent Client Service

Related titles by Law Society Publishing

Marketing, Management and Motivation
Diane Bown-Wilson and Gail Courtney

Marketing Your Law Firm
Lucy Adam

Media Relations for Lawyers
Sue Stapley

Quality Management for Law Firms
Matthew Moore

Setting Up and Managing a Small Practice
Martin Smith

Solicitors' Guide to Good Management
Trevor Boutall and Bill Blackburn

Titles from Law Society Publishing can be ordered from all good legal bookshops or direct from our distributors, Marston Book Services (tel. 01235 465656 or e-mail law.society@marston.co.uk). For further information or a catalogue, call our editorial and marketing office on 020 7320 5878.

Excellent Client Service

Strategies for Success

Heather Stewart

The Law Society

© Heather Stewart 2003

ISBN 1 85328 777 6

Published in 2003 by the Law Society
113 Chancery Lane, London WC2A 1PL

Typeset by J&L Composition, Filey, North Yorkshire
Printed by TJ International Ltd, Padstow, Cornwall

Table 10.1, p.98 reproduced by kind permission of Times Newspapers Ltd. © Times Newspapers Limited.

Contents

Introduction

> Poor performance is across the board in the profession. Of course, I see a lot of high street practices, but I also see some of the big names. Our own research shows that something like half of the firms in the country have featured in some way in a reference to this office, and that certainly includes some of the big names.[1]

Complaints are the outcome of poor client service. No firm is immune from client complaint. In fact, the larger the firm, the harder it is to ensure consistency of service delivery. Why do complaints happen? The profession claims that it looks after and cares for its clients but where does it go wrong? Delivering excellent client service has to be looked at from both sides of the coin: first, understanding what your clients actually want from a legal service and, second, how a firm goes about organising itself and motivating its people to deliver that service, the way clients want it. This book is not about complaints handling, rather it aims to be a guide to the proactive management required by practices to ensure that everyone in a firm consistently delivers a service that is valued by its clients, in terms of their confidence and value for money.

Firms are in business to provide legal services and partners want a return on their investment in the form of profits, but those profits will not come as of right. As with all businesses, it is essential that your products actually meet the requirements of the purchasers of those services, your clients. If not, they will cease to purchase. Successful firms are not complacent towards their clients. Their competitive advantage is achieved either by giving clients the added value they seek or by redesigning the way services are delivered to maintain quality levels but at the price clients are prepared to pay. They are focused, both on the client markets they are going to serve and on how they are going to serve them, profitably.

Legal services cover a very broad spectrum of activities to a very diverse range of clients. Successful client service takes place in the relationship between fee earner and client, but ensuring that it is delivered consistently, firm wide, depends upon a raft of issues:

- a clear vision of the client markets that the firm wants to serve and its strategy for doing so, including appropriate organisational structures;
- understanding what creates perceptions of both value and value for money for the clients in the markets that the firm has selected to serve;
- the leadership of the firm and its culture;

- the right mix of motivated people;
- sound financial management to ensure that the balance can be achieved between clients' needs for value for money, the needs of the firm for working capital and a level of profit;
- efficient systems and procedures that are in line with client needs to ensure a reliable and efficient service and an appropriate and effective use of IT and knowledge management to ensure that the service can be delivered efficiently and cost-effectively to the firm.

All of these have to be in tune with client needs so that the fee earner can give an excellent service to clients. This is demonstrated in the practice management model in Figure 1.1 in which the solicitor–client relationship is shown at the heart of a legal service.

The successful outcome of giving excellent service is that your clients will have confidence in your fee earners and your firm and they will perceive that they have received good value from you, both in respect of your advice and in terms of value for money. The consequences for the firm will not only be an enhanced reputation, image or brand, but also improved financial results.

It is of paramount importance that firms understand what the clients in the markets they have chosen to serve actually want from the service, at both market and individual client levels. At a market level, firms have to design the way in which their service is produced to ensure that their resources match the needs of the market, including price, and at an individual client level, value has to be created within the solicitor–client relationship. Figure 1.2 demonstrates the matching process of client needs and resources required to enable this to happen.

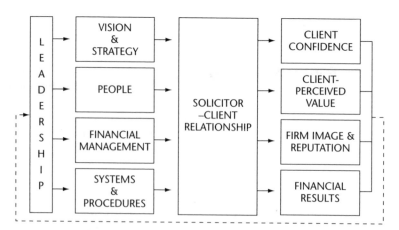

Figure 1.1   Practice management model for excellent client service
Source: Law Society *Practice Excellence,* series of CD-Roms

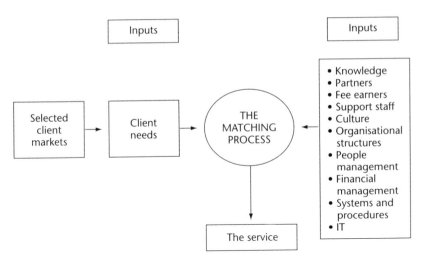

Figure 1.2   The matching process

Creating value for individual clients is not always easy for lawyers who approach the solicitor–client relationship from a different perspective to that of their client. To a fee earner, doing the work right technically is the most important issue whereas the client does not share the legal knowledge and has to assume that the work is being done correctly. Instead, depending on the level of perceived risk that the client is facing, they want confidence from their legal adviser. They also want value for money. Routine legal services are becoming increasingly price sensitive and firms have to take this into account when designing a service.

The author undertook extensive research into the value creation process for clients as part of a Ph.D. degree in legal practice management, completed in 1999. It involved both qualitative research in the form of focus groups and interviews of commercial clients and subsequent quantitative research involving a survey of the clients of 12 firms of solicitors. The benefits of the research for the profession are a greater understanding of:

- the process by which value is created for clients in the solicitor–client relationship;
- the differing natures of solicitor–client relationships across different types of clients;
- the aspects of service a client takes into account when considering the value of a legal service;
- the elements of service that lead to perceptions of value for money for clients.

The theory set out in the early chapters is based on this research and forms the foundation of much of the practical management information in subsequent chapters. Partners have to understand both what creates value for different types of clients and client markets and how that value is created, and to organise and manage their practices in such a way that their people deliver it, profitably. For many, this will involve new ways of working and perhaps the linchpin in many practices will be having a partner or partners who understand the importance of management and who have a vision of where they want their firm to be in the future. Nowadays, success does not just happen; it has to be planned and managed. There has to be a willingness to accept change and for partners to recognise that they have to have an input to the practice above and beyond legal work. Delivering excellent service is down to the people in a firm who need to be motivated to do so, from the partners to the office junior. Ensuring that work is done profitably with the right mix of fee earners, support staff and IT may involve new ways of working which are likely to involve greater teamworking. Many of the new partner responsibilities will relate to managing people, a new area for many practitioners, and one in which they will have to acquire the requisite skills. If a firm is to be successful, it has to develop its people. Commitment to client service does not mean merely paying lip-service to it; it means recognising that partners must lead by example to create a culture in which it is second nature for all to give excellent service.

This book is not a comprehensive guide to all areas of practice management. Instead it deals with the hard and soft issues necessary for the management of the delivery of excellent service from the selection of client markets, developing client relationships, seeking clients' views on service through to the implementation of any requisite changes, achieving a client-oriented culture and motivating people to accept change, financial management and managing billing, risk management and handling complaints. A further reading section is provided at the end of the book.

The book is aimed principally at partners of legal firms because, without their commitment to delivering excellent client service, work undertaken by managers and others in a firm towards achieving the firm's objectives will be largely ineffective. Research has shown that 85 per cent of lawyers fall within the controllers and/or analysers quadrant of the Myers–Briggs Indicator.[2] They are not natural entrepreneurs, and managers have to understand this and to gain partners' acceptance of the importance of client service in terms of practice development before they will give their commitment to it. It is hoped that this book will assist in achieving this.

Notes

1   A. Abraham, 'Complaints still a concern', [2002] *Gazette*, 11 July, 3.
2   B. Sabol, 'Maximising the benefits – making law firm client relationship management work', *Managing Partner*, 4(8), February 2002 p.23.

2

The role of client service in practice development

- The importance of building a firm image or brand and the importance of client service in that development
- The issues that enable the delivery of consistently excellent service
- Marketing that leads to practice development
- Understanding clients' service requirements

What is a firm's image or brand?

We all recognise the importance of image in practice development, but what is a firm's 'image' or 'brand'? Why *is* it so important? The ever increasing size of the profession and number of legal firms coupled with external threats to markets such as the availability of commodity legal services via the Internet has resulted in even greater competition and, in many fields and places, too many firms trying to provide the same range of services. But why are some firms successful and others not when in theory they operate in the same marketplace? Success lies not in being complacent, but in building an image and a competitive advantage achieved either by giving clients the added value they seek or by redesigning the way services are delivered to maintain quality levels, but at a price that clients are prepared to pay.

Unfortunately, there is no quick fix for creating an image or brand because it is the perception of a firm in the minds of its clients, potential clients, fellow professionals, professionals who refer clients, and the marketplace in general. Although clients may initially instruct a firm or a member of it because of a reputation for specific expertise, their perceptions of the quality of the service they receive consistently meeting their expectations lead to a positive experience and the consequent creation of a positive image of the firm in their minds. Image in the marketplace is an accumulation of these individual perceptions and therefore develops over time. Although profile-raising exercises to enhance awareness of the firm's expertise may be appropriate to fulfil specific marketing objectives, unless the service actually delivered is perceived to be one of quality and value to the client market, the benefits from such activities will be short lived. A firm's image tends to be relatively stable and to move incrementally, with the result that either it may take some time to catch up with improvements in service or, conversely, it may remain high for a short while even if a firm's service levels have deteriorated or no longer meet the requirements of the client market. Client markets change and firms that rest on their laurels will ultimately pay the price – they have to ensure that their image and concomitant service levels remain relevant to the markets they are serving.

Branding is not about packaging the firm, its letter heading or its logo. It comes from a firm listening to its clients to understand what they want from the firm by way of service, and from everyone in the firm not only understanding what those requirements are but actually giving a service that meets them. To do so should be second nature. Branding has been described as '. . . a shorthand for the culture of the organisation'.[1] James Dallas of Denton Wilde Sapte[2] defines culture as the attributes by which a firm identifies itself and is known outside and which reflect the way that the firm handles its clients and staff. A positive culture, as perceived by its clients, supports a firm's success to the extent that it helps to attract and retain clients and staff. Firms can create a culture; they can set the scene for the way in which the firm delivers its service to its clients, and the consistency of that service. Image, brand and reputation are derived from delivering that culture to clients.

Image and practice development

An image or brand is the principal way in which a firm can differentiate itself from its competitors and it is therefore highly influential both in attracting new business and in inspiring confidence in existing clients. Because legal services are so highly intangible and knowledge based it is very hard for potential clients to differentiate between firms. Clients, who usually have a lot at stake when they instruct a solicitor, want to make the right decision. Which is the best firm, has the most experienced and competent people and will best look after their interests? They just do not know and there is no means of telling in advance or having a trial run. Consequently for clients there is a high level of risk involved in their decision. Private clients, who usually buy legal services discretely, may have previous experience of a particular firm but often they have to rely on the recommendation of people they know and whose judgement they trust, or on referral from another professional. Commercial clients tend to have ongoing relationships with one or more firms whom they instruct according to the nature of the risk that they perceive they are facing on a 'horses for courses' basis. They also frequently select a new firm on the basis of recommendation or professional referral. Other clients, private or commercial, rely on the firm's image in the marketplace for expertise in the requisite field, or on the reputation of an individual within a firm, when making their choice.

Developing an image or brand based on excellent service is a firm's most effective marketing tool and is an opportunity open to all practices. It does not involve a large marketing budget – firms should bear in mind that it can cost up to 60 per cent more to attract a new client than to sell additional services to an existing one. Firms ranging in size from sole practitioners to over 50 partners who attended Law Society seminars on client service during 2000 reported generating up to 75 per cent of new work from repeat business or recommendation and a further 10–15 per cent from professional referrals. Figure 2.1 shows the causal sequence involved.

Surprisingly few firms use computer systems to record the source of work, despite having the facility to do so. It is a simple task to include a question on a new-matter form and to produce reports at firm, department or work-type level. Not only is the information useful for marketing purposes, but publishing the figures and comparing them across departments, where appropriate, emphasises to everyone in the firm the importance of giving excellent service to clients.

The frequently quoted tale that one unhappy client tells nine others of his/her dissatisfaction is a good reminder of the negative impact of poor service on a firm's image, particularly in private client markets. Dissatisfied clients are likely to moan to family, friends, in the hairdresser's or the pub, of any dent, however slight, in their confidence in the service they are receiving. The fee earner involved may be unaware of the dissatisfaction and the firm will certainly not realise the effect that the 'bad mouthing' is having upon its reputation. Dissatisfaction often arises from the client's lack of understanding of the legal process or of the reason their matter has taken a certain course, or from their inability to contact their solicitor, possibly because the solicior has failed to return calls. Professionals rarely understand the client's need for information to allay perceptions of risk. Greater familiarity with legal services may result in commercial clients being less likely to discuss perceived poor service from their legal representatives with others outside their organisation. They are more likely to complain or will simply stop instructing the firm.

Figure 2.1 Excellent service: a firm's most effective marketing tool

Marketing as promotion versus marketing as serving clients' needs

In recent years, practices of all sizes and types have given increased attention to general management and marketing although for many, the old misunderstanding of what 'marketing' involves still remains. Most firms feel that they do not 'do' enough 'marketing' and that they are not very effective at the little that they actually do. Each year, they vow that they will do more to attract more or better-quality work, but the good intentions and momentum only last if fee-earning work allows. 'Marketing' is put on the back burner – and stays there because fee earners are more comfortable with fee earning. Marketing initiatives therefore invariably fail because they are undertaken in a piecemeal fashion. A marketing partner may be appointed, but that partner is often expected to work miracles, alone. Even where professional marketers are employed, they are rarely given full scope in developing a practice and frequently encounter attitudes of 'we know best' from partners and fee earners.

Many firms do have a reasonable marketing budget but they do not always spend their money wisely. Time and effort are often wasted on trying to establish general name awareness of a firm and insufficient efforts are devoted to finding out what clients actually want from your firm rather than what you think they should have. Only 21 per cent of the firms in a recent survey[3] used surveys of their target markets as marketing tools. Instead marketers in those firms concentrated 85 per cent of their efforts on internal news and public relations. Firms should bear in mind that Slaughter & May has achieved magic-circle status and success without a marketing department.

Many practitioners do not appreciate that marketing goes to the heart of practice management. The 'Marketforce' survey found that 59 per cent of senior managers in the firms surveyed did not appreciate the importance of marketing as a key strategic function. The Chartered Institute of Marketing's definition of marketing is that it is 'the management process responsible for identifying, anticipating and satisfying customer requirements profitably'. Firms need to understand what message they ought to be sending out to their chosen client markets and then to implement business development plans based on communicating that message. Marketing involves changing the way the firm and the individuals within it operate to obtain the best fit between the needs of your current and potential clients and the firm's resources. Improving the way you deal with clients should be a commercial decision based on the future profitability of the firm. Firms need to be proactive to ensure that they understand their clients' needs and align the firm's organisational structures and processes to meet those needs and the expectations and perceptions of value of their clients. Solicitors pride themselves on giving a good service to clients, but excellent client service means giving a service that your clients consider excellent. In other words, a service that is excellent in client terms rather than a service that you consider excellent. First, you have to identify your clients' needs and expectations, and then work out how you are going to meet them, consistently and profitably.

The results of a survey in 1999 undertaken by Wheeler Associates and McCallum Layton of 150 firms, including 29 per cent of the top 50 practices in the country, showed that legal firms are not good at recognising the need for strategic planning when considering a firm's marketing strategy. They cited[4] problems ranging from 'insufficient focus on clients' needs' to 'under investment in marketing resources' to 'misunderstanding branding'. The survey concluded that many firms are wasting their money because they are not focusing on the marketing activities that really make a difference to attracting and retaining clients. In a survey[5] of the delegates attending the 'Strategic marketing for the legal profession' conference in 2001, the following factors were considered among the strongest that inhibit professional service firms developing a strong brand.

- Partnership structures – 71%.
- Lack of understanding of the benefits of branding – 96%.
- Lack of strong leadership – 75%.

Marketing is about talking to clients, understanding the client market and delivering what the market wants.

CHAPTER SUMMARY

1. Managers must understand that image is based on a firm consistently delivering a service that meets the expectations of the markets it has chosen to serve and that it is not built on the decor and design of an office, or on public relations.

2. Firms are in business to provide legal services and the solicitor–client relationship forms the core of them. All areas of practice management should support the delivery of that service.

3. Marketing should be based on gaining a greater understanding of the needs and expectations of each of the markets a firm has chosen to serve. Practitioners should concentrate their 'marketing' efforts on the day-to-day delivery of a service that meets those needs.

4. Marketing budgets should be used wisely. All marketing activities should be evaluated to assess their cost–benefit.

5. Firms should keep a record of the amount of repeat business and referrals.

Notes

1   Meirian Jones, Edge Ellison [2000] *Gazette*, 15 June.
2   J. Dallas, 'Culture – ingredient X', *Managing Partner*, 4(3), July/August 2001.
3   'Marketforce' [2002] *Gazette*, 25 April.
4   D. Hayes, 'Market makers', [1999] *Gazette*, 1 December.
5   H. Steen, 'Online transactional law', *Managing Partner*, 4(7), December 2001–January 2002, p.21.

Solicitor–client relationships

KEY POINTS

- The differing perspectives of solicitor and client to the relationship
- The process of creating perceptions of value
- How clients form expectations
- The differing nature of relationships with clients: private, commercial, and small owner-managed business clients
- Developing client relationships

Consistent client service

Delivering excellent service is not like doing some 'marketing'. Paying lip-service to it will not be enough. It has to happen continuously, consistently, and from every fee earner and member of staff, from the senior partner to the office junior. Everyone has to recognise its importance and his or her part in making it happen. Research has shown that even in well-managed practices, clients have inconsistent impressions of the service that they receive either from different departments or from individuals within a firm.[1] It is up to the partners of a firm to create a culture in which delivering excellent service is second nature to all and for them to lead by example. Buyers of commercial legal services are increasingly sophisticated and base their purchase decision on the perceived value of the service to their organisation. Private clients may be less sophisticated when buying legal services, but they are members of a consumerist society and look for value and anticipate a level of service. But what is value to a client? What are value-added services? In this chapter, we look at the way in which value is created for clients within the solicitor–client relationship and then, in Chapters 4 and 5, at which key elements of service create perceptions of added value and value for money.

Solicitor–client: different perspectives

Solicitors are frequently criticised for their level of client service. But ask the majority of solicitors and they would maintain that they look after their clients and do a good job for them. So why does this mismatch of perceptions exist? Perhaps it is because solicitor and client approach their relationship from quite different perspectives.

To a solicitor, satisfaction from doing a job well comes above all from doing it well technically, resolving an issue in the client's best interests, researching a point of law or drafting a complicated document that contains all relevant information in a clear and lucid manner, for example. Within the profession and individual firms, judgement of a fee earner's capabilities is based on technical skill. A potential negligence claim is seen as far worse than any delay in responding to a client. In addition, one client's matter is usually only one of many ongoing matters for numerous clients with which a fee earner is currently dealing.

Clients see legal services from a quite different viewpoint. For them, your technical ability is assumed – they do not share your knowledge and have not spent several years qualifying and practising to gain your expertise and experience. That is the service they buy from you. Clients frequently instruct a solicitor over a matter that is of great importance to them and when they consider your service they want to feel confident that they are receiving the best advice and that they are paying a price for your service which they consider reasonable and cost-effective for them, in other words that they are receiving good value from you. An assessment of value is a personal judgement made about a firm's service by a client after they have experienced that service. Price, value for money, also plays a part in the assessment, but it is considered separately. Thus, there are effectively two strands in the process of the creation of value: first, aspects of service leading to the creation of trust and confidence in the relationship between solicitor and client and, second, perceived value for money. The emphasis placed on each will vary with each client across matters depending on their perception of the risk they are facing. We now consider what lies behind the creation of perceptions of both.

Value for clients

A client's perception of the value of your service is actually the reality for that individual. Value has to reflect what the client has gained but making that assessment in respect of our knowledge-based services is not easy or straightforward for them. We have seen that their initial purchase decision is problematic and that existing and potential clients have to trust that members of their chosen firm have the requisite technical skills to solve their problem, before they even instruct them.

Their difficulties continue. Clients cannot judge the correctness of your advice even after the work has been completed and can usually only tell if it has been incorrect if something goes wrong in the future. Nor can they rely on the outcome of the matter as a measure of the service. They may be unsuccessful in achieving their objectives, despite being satisfied that you could not have done more for them. Therefore clients approach legal services with perceptions of risk – whether you actually have the right experience and judgemental skills and they have made their selection wisely, of their chance of success, of the potential cost. For them, it is uncharted territory. They do not feel in control, *they* do not have the knowledge and this manifests itself in their need for information from you. Imagine how you would feel if you were awaiting the results of medical tests and the desire you would feel to contact your consultant or GP to obtain the information you want. What *all* clients want, whether commercial, corporate or private, however funded, is confidence and peace of mind. They want to move their own business forward or to get on with their lives and they want you to handle their matter as effectively as possible to achieve their aims. This need for confidence and the trust that is generated in the solicitor–client relationship distinguishes it from many other services.

If clients do not know whether your advice is accurate, what does generate their confidence in you and your firm? They have to trust that you have the requisite technical expertise and, instead, they rely on the aspects of your service that they can evaluate – the way you manage their matter, actually deliver the advice and perform the service for them, and are genuinely interested in them and their concerns. These are the most important elements of legal service and provide the greatest source of client confidence and consequent added value. They place much greater emphasis on *how* the service is provided rather than *what* is provided and a service that successfully meets a client's needs is viewed even more positively if the client perceives it to be as a result of a fee earner's efforts. Here, small matters can play a large part: delivering a document by hand to ensure that it arrives on time; keeping a client informed, even if only to report that no progress has been made.

The way a fee earner manages the relationship with a client is crucial in developing client confidence. But it is a two-way process. You cannot produce the service without your client whose instructions you need and, although you are in control, you have to manage the relationship to the client's satisfaction. Do not forget that it is up to the client and not the firm as to whether or not the purchase of a legal service is made and whether the relationship continues. The perceived value of your service will be totally subjective to your client. Fee earners cannot customise technical knowledge, but they can customise how they give the advice and manage a matter. It is therefore up to a fee earner to understand an individual client's needs and to meet them. A dissatisfied client is far more likely to be dissatisfied with how the advice is delivered rather than the advice itself.

Although the fee earner is at the spearhead of the service, good support staff, an effective use of IT, good financial management, office systems and procedures and case management systems all help you to deliver a reliable, timely and efficient service, as shown in Figure 3.1. Everyone in the practice should appreciate the importance of the role they play in the team effort in creating client confidence in the fee earner and in the firm.

Although first impressions are important, do not delude yourself into thinking that a smart reception area and friendly receptionist are sufficient to create value for a client. Client confidence is *created* by your performance of the service and only enhanced by other secondary aspects of service that do not become important unless there is something lacking in them. Every encounter that a client has with your firm is taken into account in their evaluation of the service. The importance of the service to the client means that a single contact with the firm can radically affect the overall relationship to the extent that it can be deepened or broken off altogether. One interaction that the client feels has not met expectations may prejudice the client's overall evaluation. Each 'moment of truth' is a chance to get the service right, or to get it wrong, an opportunity to enhance their initial trust or to erode or destroy it completely. Unfortunately you do not get a second go. Everyone within a firm should understand the effects of failing to manage client expectations in such a way so that the service delivered at least matches them.

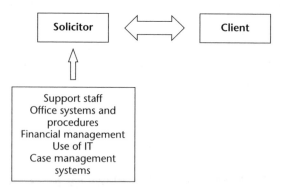

Figure 3.1   The solicitor–client relationship

Value for money

In addition to assessing the extent of their confidence in the firm and the advice given, clients also assess value for money – the price they are paying. In general terms, the greater the clients' perception of the risk they face, the more they are prepared to pay for perceived expertise and experience.

Your relationship with your client is quite different in their assessment of value for money. Trust and confidence no longer form the root of it, although if you mishandle the elements of service that create confidence, you can erode or destroy all the good efforts you have put into building the relationship. Instead, clients regard you as they would any other contractor of services and they are unable to understand, and sometimes misconstrue, solicitors' reluctance to discuss costs. This has an impact on perceptions of value for money but, as busy practitioners, we frequently forget or underestimate the feelings of risk and uncertainty that clients bring to a legal service. Clients are fearful of the potential cost of legal services and want as much information as we can possibly give at the beginning of a matter. Indeed, commercial clients who have ongoing relationships with their legal advisers often insist on total transparency of billing and for matters to be billed strictly in accordance with their agreement with the firm. That is what all clients would like, but few receive. Clients are worried about high fees, hidden costs and surprises, and costs that escalate outside their control. For some reason, many solicitors are more afraid than their clients when it comes to talking about money but clients *need* to know about costs, not only at the outset but throughout a matter so that element of their uncertainty can be resolved.

The process of creating both strands of value for all clients is demonstrated in Figure 3.2.

Trust exists at the outset and develops over time through the confidence that the client has in your service, created by the way in which you perform the key elements of it. Price is a separate strand in the process. It has a direct impact on perceptions of value, but these can be totally destroyed if the key elements of service do not meet expectations. Together, confidence in you and your service, and value for money, create perceptions of value. Whatever the level of expertise delivered,

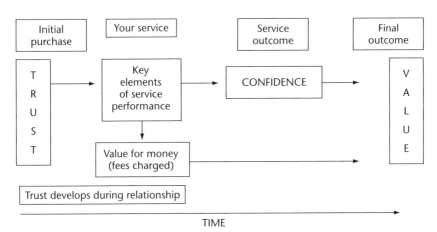

Figure 3.2 Client evaluation of legal services

perceptions of value depend on the client's *own experience* of your service and whether their previous expectations of certain key elements of it have been met. Although some clients are extremely sophisticated users of legal services, others may be instructing a solicitor for the first time. What are your client's expectations of your service and what will provide value in a particular matter?

Clients' expectations

That clients expect too much nowadays and no longer show any respect for lawyers is a common cry from practitioners around the country. Clients are demanding, they want everything done yesterday, they are constantly on the phone, but they want to pay less and less for your services. How can you give such clients a service that they are satisfied with and yet still make a reasonable level of profit and have a life outside work for yourself? But what are clients' expectations, where do they originate, and how are they formed?

Expectations play a key part in the evaluation process by clients. They are formed as a result of a process that is particularly complex in the case of highly intangible legal services. Every client has a different script and unique expectations. For first-time users of our services, usually private clients, expectations may not even be completely formed. They may have been told about what to expect by family or friends, but have never actually experienced a professional service. The client will not necessarily be able to specify his or her expectations beforehand, but will be aware immediately if they are not being met. Clients may have different expectations when interacting with different parts of your service, for example clients may appreciate the warm and reassuring manner of a receptionist but that is not nearly as important to them as a fee earner with whom they feel that they can communicate. In addition, expectations can change over time, even within the same matter, after your client has had experience of your service or a change in their own circumstances, for instance. Figure 3.3 sets out the issues that can have an impact, to a greater or lesser extent, on a client's expectations of you and your firm.

- *Word of mouth*: messages received by clients from colleagues, family, friends for instance about you, your firm and your service and what you have achieved for them, will influence what they expect from you.
- *Marketing communications*: marketing communications sent out by the firm itself similarly influence expectations. Stating that you are experts in a field of law will result in clients anticipating a breadth and depth of expertise in the area. Claiming that you are friendly and caring will result in clients expecting that of you. Their expectations

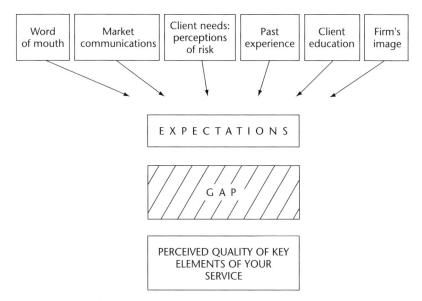

Figure 3.3 The formation of a client's expectations

will be crushed instantly if your manner is cold or uninterested, by taking phone calls during the interview for instance. Think about the effect your body language is having on your client – your mind might not be elsewhere but are you giving the impression that it is?

- *Client needs*: a client's own personal need for confidence from the relationship, generated by their perception of the risk they are facing, will impact on his or her view of the way your service is given. If you meet the client's need for information and give him or her the impression that you are pulling out all the stops for him or her, then confidence will be enhanced. However, if you give the client the impression that the client's matter is not important to you, these needs will not be met and the client's confidence will not develop. At the other end of the spectrum, some clients, both private and commercial, view some legal services as commodities. Their needs will differ from those of the client facing perceived high risk.
- *Past experience*: clients who have experienced your service before, or have been satisfied clients of other firms, will anticipate a similar level of service again, whether from the same or a different fee earner.
- *Client education*: if you inform clients at the outset of a matter about the type and level of service they will receive, they will obviously expect you to meet or exceed your promises. For example if you agree to interim-bill a client at regular intervals and you fail to do so as agreed, it is not only viewed as unreliability by your client but may also be taken as a sign that your service is inefficient in other areas.

Above all, their expectations will not be met and their confidence in you will be eroded.

- *Image*: image, brand or reputation in the marketplace will influence client expectations. The way in which you are seen by professional contacts, whose views may be based on feedback from clients whom they have previously referred to your firm, and the consequent messages they pass on to potential clients are instrumental in forming expectations.

Whatever lies behind the formation of clients' expectations, if your service does not match the quality that they expect, client confidence will not be created and your service will not deliver the anticipated and hoped-for value. The result will be a dissatisfied client. Client education is one of your most powerful tools in managing their expectations. These expectations may be unrealistic, but it is up to you to let your client know what they can expect of you and what is likely to happen in their matter. However, you cannot assume that you know what a client wants or expects from any situation, and if you do not listen to them, you will never find out.

Relationships with clients

The nature of the solicitor–client relationship differs across private and commercial clients. Small, owner-managed businesses are more akin to private clients in that they are usually less familiar with legal services and have perceptions of personal risk when instructing solicitors. Although there are key elements of service performance common to all groups, commercial clients evaluate an important additional factor as well. These key elements are covered in the next chapter. In the next section we look at the different nature of the solicitor–client relationships.

Private clients

Relationships with private clients are developed on a discrete basis over a period of years, for a conveyance, a will, a divorce for instance and they are dependent on the trust and confidence that a client develops in you. It is important to remember that every contact clients have with you is a chance to develop their confidence and to enhance their trust – or to weaken it.

A lot of your private clients will be unfamiliar with legal services or the processes involved and therefore will not know what to expect. Their feelings of risk may be exacerbated by their own emotional state that may only allow them to see their situation subjectively and may affect their ability to take in what you are saying to them, a factor that can be easily overlooked if you are constantly under pressure. This unfamiliarity with what could or should happen often makes them feel out of control of the situation. The matter is likely to be of extreme importance to the client, and it will therefore be uppermost in their mind. Fee earners must appreciate clients' consequent need for information, involve them in decisions being made as to how a case is to progress and manage their expectations. Clients need to know what to expect from your service and the likely outcome of their case, at the outset and at key stages during it.

Private clients need to be shown that you care about them and their concerns and that you are genuinely interested in them – then they will feel able to talk to you. They should not leave your office wishing that they had asked other questions or told you about some other factor, or feel dissatisfied because their matter is moving on but not necessarily the way they want it to go. You must be proactive in the relationship by letting them know what is happening and by demonstrating that you are putting effort into their work. It is usually too late in the client's eyes if the client has to chase you for information. That is not to deny that a small minority of clients appear to require excessive contact. The expectations of these clients may need to be politely but firmly managed, and they should be told of the cost of the numerous calls to the firm. Unless publicly funded, private clients are greatly concerned about the cost of your services and they need information about potential costs, not just at the beginning but also throughout a matter. You may have to explain your reasons for being unable to provide a firm estimate or fixed price in some circumstances. How to discuss costs and billing issues with clients is covered in Chapter 6.

If you remember the percentage of work that you receive from repeat business or recommendation/referral, it is certainly worthwhile looking after each and every client. Unfortunately, the majority of private clients will not let you know that they are unhappy with the way things are going – but they will tell others which, as we have seen, impacts on the image of a firm. Interestingly, the longer running a case, the less likely it is that your client will feel he or she has received value from you. According to a survey of recent users of solicitors' services conducted in 2000,[2] 48 per cent of clients whose cases had taken over 12 months to complete were dissatisfied with the time taken. This may be because of the nature of the case, matrimonial or litigation for example in which the client may not have achieved the initial hoped-for outcome. Alternatively, it may be that fee earners are not good at proactively communicating with clients on a longer-term basis.

Because private clients do not have the same 'set up' costs faced by commercial clients when establishing a relationship with a new firm, some can be very fickle and switch solicitors readily. For others, being able to say 'my solicitor' gives them an element of confidence and they are pleased to be associated with you.

Commercial/corporate clients

Again, it is important to recognise the potential mismatch of solicitor–client perceptions of the relationship and to understand what your client wants from your service. Solicitor–commercial/corporate client relationships are tenuous – they involve an ongoing evaluation by clients and need to be continuously nurtured by you. These clients are likely to have an ongoing relationship with at least one, and usually with two or three firms whom they instruct according to the type and level of technical expertise they perceive they need. They are aware of the comparative cost of legal services to the costs of production in their own business and are concerned with obtaining cost-effective legal services. They will be prepared to pay the rates of City firms if they consider that it will give them the 'clout' and confidence they need in negotiations but the same client will not pay those rates for work they consider to be of a more routine nature. Some clients will use one firm for the bulk of their work, usually a large firm because they believe that the depth and spread of expertise in such firms reduces their risk, but others, even large clients, will instruct smaller practices if they believe that the technical skill and level of service are there.

Commercial/corporate clients consider that technical skills form the core of legal services but they too assume that you have fee earners with the requisite level of competence as given. There are always other firms from whom they could obtain the same services, so why should they choose you? What can you offer them? Can you help them to achieve success in their business? Are you genuinely interested in them to the extent that you are prepared to learn about their business, so that your advice is totally relevant to it and to the commercial parameters within which they have to operate? Clients want advice that is practical and is focused on allowing them to achieve their objectives. Do you really understand those objectives and do you really share your client's ambition for success? Commercial clients' confidence is derived from their perceptions of receiving 'good advice at a cost-effective price'. The receipt of 'the best advice' lies at the heart of the solicitor–client relationship and depends on the efforts you put into understanding their business and giving advice in terms that match its needs. Can you say that you *really* understand the businesses of your clients? Do you regularly ask them about changes they have experienced, either internally within their business or in respect of the issues it faces, or the industry generally?

> I get the feeling that they very much care about your business and value the business even though it's comparatively small perhaps. Yes, it does seem to be important.
>
> I wasted quite a lot of time explaining matters that relate specifically to our business because they don't necessarily know our business.

> They come out to visit you at work, they're learning at the same time. They're not just doing a job but they're finding out about you and your business.

Some lawyers are commercial creatures, but for others it can be very hard to break free from professional constraints and to deliver advice in commercial terms. The training that solicitors receive emphasises technical competence and solicitors judge fellow members of the profession on their expertise. The majority of the profession have not experienced responsible work in a commercial environment and many find it difficult to view life from their client's perspective. Some firms encourage their fee earners to take an MBA degree to broaden their commercial awareness and others arrange for their members to be seconded into a client's business for a period. Most practitioners do not enjoy the luxury of the time required for either, but going out to a client's place of business and learning about how it operates can pay tremendous dividends on two counts: first, from the ability to deliver advice that is of greater value to the client and, second, clients really appreciate it. They view your effort as a pro-active step in developing both the relationship and their confidence. They feel valued and that their instructions are appreciated.

Developing relationships can begin before a new client instructs you. It is safe to say that few solicitors are natural salespeople and most dread being told that they must 'target' prospective clients. New clients will only buy your services if, and when, they need them and if they are motivated to do so. Hard selling will rarely produce that motivation – telling them how wonderful you are and all that you have done for other clients will probably have the opposite of the desired effect. What clients really want to know is what is in it for them – how are you going to be able to provide the services to meet their needs any better than your competitors? You are not going to win a beauty parade by merely listing your own virtues. You will stand a far greater chance if you find out as much as you can about the client's business, the key issues it faces, visit them to find out how they operate, and base any presentation on the needs of their business. Sow the seeds of the relationship even before they instruct you by showing a genuine interest.

Much has been said of the role of 'personal chemistry' in relationships, but its importance again depends upon the client. Clients have to feel at ease with their advisers to be able to communicate with them fully. To some clients, it is essential that there is a rapport that may develop into friendship. They want to get on with the person with whom they may have to spend long hours in negotiations or meetings. For others, respect for the solicitors' ability and judgement is sufficient. Firms often allocate a considerable portion of their marketing budget to social activities with clients and while these may be beneficial in strengthening relationships, a greater deepening of the relationship is likely to be achieved by you spending time at the client's place of business to gain a better understanding of it. Your advice will be more practical and commercially relevant, and therefore of greater value to the client, as a result. You can demonstrate your interest by giving your client pieces of relevant commercial information, by sending them an article they may not have seen that relates to their markets, for example.

In fact, firms' marketing budgets are often wasted on high-profile social events at which partners remain at one end of the room and clients network among themselves at the other, but the event does little to develop relationships or to attract new work. On the other hand, entertaining clients to an in-house lunch, either with members of a team or other partners present, will be of greater benefit to the relationship, providing you use the opportunity to find out more about the clients and how you can help them with their business rather than giving a sales pitch. Introducing clients to other members of your team demonstrates your depth of expertise and allows you to explore whether there are any ways in which service can be improved. Clients also feel more comfortable if they can put a face to the voice of another member of the team on the phone if the relevant fee earner is not available. By introducing clients to partners who are specialists in different fields, you are less likely to find that the client has instructed another firm because the client was unaware that you offered the particular service.

Clients also want to receive proactive advice on changes in legislation that are relevant to them. Some enjoy attending seminars, but not if the presenter merely recites the terms of new legislation. Clients want to know the practical implications of such changes in the law – they are paying you to interpret the statute. Other clients consider the content of seminars too generic for their needs or they feel they are too busy to attend and would rather you phoned or e-mailed to let them know of changes. In every case, you have to find out how your client wants you to deliver the service. Discussions as to what clients perceive as value and on the way in which the service is to be given, including costs and methods of billing, should be viewed as a means of deepening relationships with clients and as fruitful marketing exercises.

The nature of the solicitor–commercial client relationship varies across clients. Some want their legal advisers to be part of their team, to be a sounding board, while others feel that introducing solicitors at too early a stage in their negotiations complicates issues. They only want solicitors to put words around what they have already agreed. It is up to you to establish the nature of relationship that the client seeks. With some clients, it will vary according to the type of work and perceived risk involved. For clients who instruct firms solely to handle process-driven matters of a routine, commodity nature the key elements of service are likely to be efficiency, effectiveness and price. They are likely to prescribe the way in which you give the service and to be unforgiving if you do not deliver exactly what they want.

The relationship will also depend on the number of members of the client organisation who instruct the firm. If there are numerous buyers of legal services within the client organisation, the relationship with a particular partner is likely to be less strong than if only one buyer were involved. The individuals who instruct solicitors will usually be familiar with legal services and are unlikely to be emotionally involved in the issues.

Although some clients only want to deal with one partner, the demand for specialisation is now such that clients recognise that they will receive advice from several partners and fee earners in a firm. For the firm, this has advantages and disadvantages. It obviously provides greater opportunities for cross-selling services and reduces the risk of one partner or a team taking valuable clients if that partner or team leaves a firm. A downside is ensuring consistency of service levels across the fee earners. A 'relationship' partner is usually required to ensure not only that the client's functional requirements are met, but also that the client has confidence in all the partners and fee earners who undertake their work. Problems can also arise if the client does not get on with the relationship partner. Firms need a mechanism available to clients that lets them report back any loss of confidence – it is not worth losing the client over an issue of which the person may be unaware. This is not the same as a formal complaints procedure and can be an informal arrangement. It is often best achieved by a second tier of contact between the client, the managing or senior partner for example.

Commercial clients are reluctant to change solicitors because of the 'set up' costs involved on their part and not knowing whether a new firm will perform better. They consider that they too put effort into the relationship and are unlikely to switch firms as long as they have confidence that your firm can offer the range and depth of expertise they require, and that you will give them 'the best advice' and the level of service they require. However, if they feel that you are becoming complacent towards them and perhaps taking their work for granted, even in small, low-value matters, they are likely to take all or part of their business elsewhere.

> They are not as responsive – I think that they have become a little complacent about their position.

> If there's a certain amount of complacency and if you're dealing with them over a number of years, slowly the goodwill will erode.

Your service should be planned to meet clients' needs and to ensure that their expectations are either met or managed to an appropriate level. Remember that commercial clients change and develop over time and what they want from a relationship consequently changes. Doing what you have done for the last 20 years will not necessarily meet the current needs of your clients. You have to keep abreast of their needs and their business. Discussing their business, how you can better help them to achieve their objectives and the level and type of service they want from you is not remotely unprofessional – if you fail to do this, your client is likely to stop instructing you.

Small, owner-managed business clients

Owner-managed businesses are a hybrid of private and corporate/commercial clients and, unless they are looked after, they can easily be dissatisfied with the service they receive. It can be difficult to combine working for large client organisations and this segment of the market. These clients are likely to instruct solicitors on a less frequent basis than larger commercial organisations whose spending power they do not share. Their personal confidence may not be sufficient to enable them to express their dissatisfaction to the firm or to specify the service levels they want. They tend to stick with one firm loyally for some time and they may be reluctant to leave it despite not being totally happy with the firm's service because 'better the devil you know'. Their strong sense of personal interest in the business and their financial stake in it results in them being emotionally involved. The needs of these clients should not be overlooked: from little acorns, oak trees grow. They need you to demonstrate a strong and genuine interest in their business whose success is very personal to them. They need you to understand the commercial problems they face and the structure of the markets within which they operate because they often rely on their legal adviser for business guidance.

CHAPTER SUMMARY

1.   There must be a general awareness on the part of everyone in a firm of the underlying needs of different groups of clients and of the perceptions of risk they bring to the service.

2.   Partners and managers *must* understand the roles that confidence and trust play in the client evaluation process. It forms an integral part of the solicitor–client relationship and should be stressed to *all* members of a firm.

3.   Managing expectations begins before the client instructs a firm. Messages sent out should be in line with the needs of the markets it serves and a firm should not overpromise.

4.   Careful consideration should be given to the competencies upon which appraisals and bonus systems are based. Commercial acumen should be included for fee earners undertaking commercial work.

5.   Fee earners need training to ensure that they are aware of:

(a)   the different perceptions of the service between solicitor and client;

(b)   the perceived risks that clients bring to the service;

(c)   the need to listen to clients to be aware of their expectations and to manage them appropriately, if required;

(d)   the issues that lie behind the creation of trust and confidence and that lead to perceptions of value and of value for money;

(e)   the importance of understanding the nature of a client's business and demonstrating that they take it into account when giving advice.

6.   Managers should be aware of potential inconsistencies of service delivery between fee earners and ensure that all fee earners are aware of the dangers of perceived complacency by clients.

7.   Partners should recognise the importance of developing relationships with commercial clients through demonstrating a genuine interest in the client and in their business.

8.   Firms should proactively seek clients' views on levels of service both overall and for individual commercial clients.

Notes

1   H. M. Stewart (1999): 'The evaluation of legal services by commercial and corporate clients – implications for service design and delivery', Ph.D. thesis, University of Bradford.
2   'Client experiences: A survey of recent users of solicitors' services', prepared for the Research and Policy Planning Unit of the Law Society of England and Wales by BRMB International, December 2000.

Creating confidence and value for clients

KEY POINTS

- Your technical skills are assumed: it is *how* you deliver the service that creates value
- The elements of service that do create value for clients
- Producing a legal service is a two-way process: listen to your clients and involve them
- For commercial clients, real value comes from the commercial practicality of your advice; understand your client's business

Key service performance factors

In Chapter 3, we saw that there are two strands in the creation of value for clients: creating trust and confidence through the way in which the service is given, and perceptions of value for money. We look first at the key elements of your service that create confidence and consider what lies behind perceptions of value for money in Chapter 5. In view of clients' perceptions of risk and their lack of knowledge about what could or should happen, anything that reduces that uncertainty will increase their confidence and add value for them. There are several interlinked elements of your service that generate confidence and have a direct influence on creating value for clients. These key elements are obviously the ones on which you should concentrate your efforts to meet, and preferably exceed, your client's expectations. They are not always the easiest to manage because they involve the behaviours of individual fee earners and managers of practices cannot lay down rules or procedures for the management of human relationships. Nor are managers aware of what passes in a client–fee earner interaction. All fee earners should themselves be aware of the danger of clients' perceptions of complacency and managers should monitor clients' views of the firm's service to ensure that any problems are rectified as soon as possible.

In the last chapter, we saw that the nature of the solicitor–client relationship varies across groups of clients. Although there are common elements that create value for all clients, corporate/commercial clients also derive value from the commercial practicality of legal advice and we shall look at that later in this chapter. The key elements for *all* clients as shown in Figure 4.1 are:

- your technical skills, even though these have to be assumed;
- your honesty and integrity, which are also taken as read;
- your communication skills, including your listening skills, how you communicate and how often you communicate;
- your responsiveness, promptness of action and timeliness of advice;
- your accessibility and how easily clients can contact you for advice;
- your reliability, efficiency, attention to detail, how often you do what you say you will and actually ensure that work accords with your client's instructions;
- the way in which you demonstrate to a client that you value both the client's work and the client;
- the professional approach of everyone in the firm.

To some practitioners, these may appear old chestnuts, but research[1] has now shown that they lie at the root of the creation of client value and satisfaction. Unless you can guarantee consistency of service in your practice, they need to be reiterated time and again because a breakdown on any one of them can cause a loss of client confidence and lower perceived value. The quoted extracts given in this book are comments made by clients during focus groups or interviews conducted by the author over a period of years. The clients involved were familiar with legal services – consider how a first-time user of legal services must feel.

Technical skills

Clients have to base their belief that you are competent either on their own past experience of your service or on your image and reputation for expertise in a specific area. This applies to all clients. Commercial clients, for example, usually value the reassurance provided by the range and depth of expertise offered by larger firms. Although your technical ability has to be assumed, clients, particularly those familiar with legal services, can tell very quickly if a fee earner is out of his or her depth which obviously leads to a rapid diminution of client confidence in that person. Never try to pull the wool over a client's eyes: do not accept instructions when you do not have the competence to deal with the matter.

Conversely, client confidence is enhanced if fee earners admit that they do not have certain specific knowledge.

> It's quite plain the partner they have is out of his depth and we just did not have the confidence and we used another firm altogether.

A good contractor will recognise when he is out of his depth and will say to a client – stop! I must get a specialist or you should get a specialist to advise you on this.

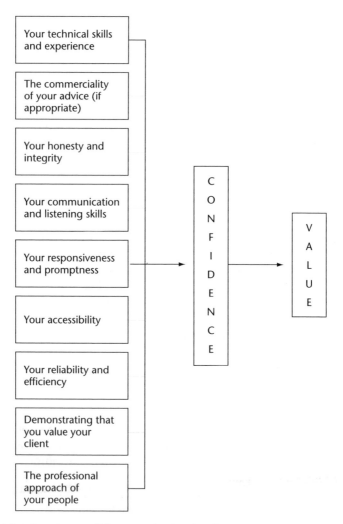

Figure 4.1   Creating confidence and value for clients

Clients also value your knowledge of the subject area of a matter. For example, a commercial client will be grateful if you actually visit a property so that your enquiries are appropriate and cover all relevant aspects.

Two-way communication

Because creating a legal service is a two-way process, communication is of paramount importance. The following comment summarises what clients want from their solicitor.

> Someone you can explain the situation to and they understand in your language, synthesise and come back to you and say, right, this is what you can do, in English. You want to understand what they are going to do and what it's going to cost you and that's really important.

You and your client must share the same interpretation of your client's objectives, in respect of both *what* the client wants to happen and *how* they want it to happen. Commercial clients whose matters are of the process-based commodity type will doubtless instruct you as to how to undertake their work. Most other clients will rely on your judgement on the way their matter is to be conducted but that is not to say they do not want to be involved and to have their opinion sought. You are in the driving seat in the relationship, but clients do not want to feel out of control. Involve them in the way the matter is to progress, at the outset and throughout. 'Don't worry, leave it all to me', is not necessarily going to engender the level of confidence you anticipate. All too often, fee earners assume that they know a client's objectives in a situation without giving the client the opportunity to discuss what they really want. Consider whether you have discussed the issues fully and whether your client really understands why they cannot achieve the result that they had hoped for. Let clients know how what you are doing benefits them and their case. Emphasise the value of what you are doing for them. Agree a plan for the course the matter is to take up to each stage. Consult the client whenever there needs to be a change of plan. Your client should always understand what you together are trying to achieve from any course of action. Both the Legal Services Commission Contracting Specifications and the Law Society's Practice Management Standards contain requirements for case planning with clients for this purpose.

You also have to make sure that your client understands your advice. This may seem a very elementary step, but clients do not like to ask what you mean because they do not wish to feel foolish – this also applies to well-educated clients. Too often clients have the perception that solicitors intentionally fail to use straightforward language. Obviously, this is not the case but we forget that clients do not have the benefit of legal training and are rarely familiar with legal processes or terminology. What does a disbursement mean to a client, discovery of documents or even a local authority search? Everyday terms, but not ones with which your client is necessarily familiar.

> They talk in 'law' words, don't they? They don't make it very clear to you what they all mean.

They create work for themselves because they make everything so complex, so inaccessible to the ordinary person, it's like a closed shop. The Law is designed to be beyond your reach.

They like to leave you standing because they know the law and they'll use legal terms that leave you totally confused.

Listening skills

Communication is a two-way process. Solicitors are used to being in control, to giving advice and to being the person who does the talking. They are not always good at listening. However, the ability to *listen* and understand what a client actually wants is essential.

You have got to listen to the person and he/she has got to listen to you – that's the most important thing.

We won't instruct him again. We'll find someone who really does listen to you – that's the most important thing.

You have to give the lawyer the background. They have to understand. But a lot of lawyers are just not interested in listening to anybody else.

You have to ensure that you understand what your client does want by listening and by making sure from your own behaviour that the client feels sufficiently at ease to give full instructions. You might consider this statement elementary but why do so many clients, commercial and private, think that solicitors do not listen?

Listening is a skill. Getting the full picture involves asking open questions, 'tell me a bit more about . . .'. 'Can you explain a bit more fully why you think that . . .'. Summarising and reflecting back what the client has said during the interview is a helpful way of ensuring that you have understood and gives them an opportunity to fill in any gaps. It also enables you to make sure that your client has understood you and that you are both on the same wavelength. Your body language also influences whether clients feel able to open up to you. Sitting back in a chair, fiddling with paper clips, avoiding eye contact all signify a lack of interest to your client. Giving them your undivided attention and making appropriate comments such as '. . . go on' and '. . . I see' show that you are taking on board what your client is telling you.

I can't speak highly enough of the group of solicitors I was put in touch with. The particular lady that I saw was first rate . . . she had loads of time to spend with me, she didn't rush me, she had to do drawings of the situation and how the injury occurred and she didn't rest until she was sure she knew everything about how the injury had occurred.

She always had time for me. She was such a help.

The Law Society's series of CD-Roms entitled *Practice Excellence* (available from Law Society Business Centre) contain filmed examples of interviewing and communication skills to ensure that your client will leave an interview feeling satisfied, not necessarily with the potential outcome of their case, but with the way in which you are handling it.

Agreeing how to communicate

Establish a communication agreement at the outset – when and how: e-mail, phone, letter or fax. Do not be afraid of suggesting e-mail to all clients, regardless of age group. If you have never talked about it with a longstanding client, ask the client for his or her views at any time – they will welcome it. Whichever method is chosen, clients should perceive that it is the fastest available. Reporting information to your client can be on a routine basis, or in respect of a new development or change of plan. Updates can be simple or complicated. However, as clients need to understand the content and even when they do they rarely have the time to go through complex issues, the more simple and succinct the better. Many commercial/corporate clients prefer reports on key issues on a single sheet of A4, using bullet points. Sending a client a copy letter received from the other side and asking for instructions may move it from your desk but it does not create value for your client. Instead summarise the contents of the letter, and their implications, and suggest options with the relevant pros and cons for the client to consider. Some clients resent receiving confirmatory letters because of the cost, but there obviously has to be a balance between the client's needs and those of the firm in protecting itself. Explain that you need to keep a full record and that your letters confirm that you have interpreted instructions accurately.

Agreeing who is to be involved

If more than one fee earner is to be involved in the matter, let the client know who they are and which aspects of the work each fee earner will undertake. Even better, introduce the client to each fee earner. Practitioners argue that teamworking does not work for some areas. Other firms make it happen. For example, some solicitors do not accept that family matters can be handled by more than one person because of the importance of the solicitor–client relationship when the client is in an emotional state. Others undertake family work very successfully in teams of up to four but more often of two people. Clients are told that a paralegal will deal with the initial stages but that as soon as issues become complicated, the file will be passed across to the person with experience. By using IT effectively everyone in the team can access the file and respond to the client's queries if the main fee earner is unavailable. As long as the client is informed at the outset and fee earners have the will to make it work, it can. The client should be notified of any changes in the arrangements or in fee earners, preferably before they occur.

Being responsive

Commercial clients in particular look for speed of response in receiving advice. Private clients are motivated by things they understand: receiving regular progress reports or the fee earner returning a phone call promptly. All phone calls should be returned within 24 hours, without exception, either by the fee earner concerned or by someone with the relevant knowledge of the matter. It gives clients a greater impression of your responsiveness than anything else. To a client who does not understand legal processes and to whom the matter is of the utmost importance, any delay in receiving information can lead to a perception that something is wrong. Any lack of response merely heightens the client's uncertainty and the fact that a letter is waiting to be typed does not alleviate it. Different interpretations of timing can add to the uncertainty. Even when a client says that a matter is not urgent, they do not intend that it should be constantly placed at the bottom of the pile. When the client has not heard after several weeks, they are likely to feel very dissatisfied.

> You shouldn't be expected to be on the phone every two or three weeks – what stage are we at? I find that very irritating.

> Even if they are specialists, they say, oh yes, we'll do that and then you wait weeks and weeks for some action.

Being proactive is very beneficial to the relationship with your client. Keeping in touch regularly, even if there is nothing to report, ensures they are aware that the reason for any delay does not lie at your door and that you are involving them.

There can be inconsistency in levels of service across fee earners in the same firm, despite good management in other areas. The following example involved a firm with several offices that has both Investors in People and Lexcel accreditation. A potential client phoned one office to be told that the appropriate fee earner for the type of matter worked from another office and he should phone there. The potential client did so on two occasions over a few days and each time requested that the fee earner ring him back, but the calls were not returned. He rang a third time almost a week later and finally managed to speak to the fee earner. His views of the firm's responsiveness and efficiency and his own confidence in the firm were tainted by this introduction. To the fee earner, the phone call was probably one on a list of many, some of which he managed to return in an extremely busy day, but that is no excuse for failing to respond to the second call. To a client, two or three days are a long time when the matter is uppermost in their mind.

Even if the fee earner just does not have time or is away from the office, a firm should have a system for holding calls to be made either by a secretary or receptionist. In firms without support staff, fee earners have no back-up and it is even more important that they understand the need to return calls promptly. Beware, too, of the dangers of voice mail. Although it is extremely useful in ensuring that fee earners receive accurate messages from clients, managers should be aware that some fee earners do not always respond to messages.

Being available to clients

There will be numerous times when a fee earner cannot be available to a client, for example, if you are in court every day from 10.00 a.m. to 4.30 p.m. Tell your client that there is no point in phoning you between these times. Let clients know when you will be in a position to ring back – and do so. If you have competent support staff, explain to the client that the person can probably deal with the query or take a reliable message. Introducing the member of staff helps to give the client confidence in that person. A word of warning – make sure that your secretary does not come across as being a gatekeeper guarding access to you. They can be overly protective and need to remember that unfortunately clients' interests come before your own. Support staff play a more important role in their direct contact with private clients than with commercial/corporate clients. The latter usually only want to speak to the relevant fee earner whereas most private clients are quite happy to speak to competent support staff – perhaps they perceive it may cost them less.

Clients want to feel they can get hold of their fee earner and firms should ensure that their switchboard hours are convenient for their client markets. The odd firm still closes at lunchtime, which is hard to understand when most of their clients probably work and perhaps the only time they can contact their solicitor is during their own lunch hour. Beware also of too many levels in a switchboard – clients often have limited time. They do not like to have to go through a switchboard, a department and a secretary before they reach the fee earner. It is even more galling if a voice mail message lies at the end of their wait. Consider your clients when designing your systems.

Being reliable

> Frankly all the things that you would expect from a supplier of widgets. On the right day, in the right packages, as you've instructed them, literally.

This sums up what clients want from a firm in terms of its reliability, internal efficiency and effectiveness. Perceptions of a fee earner's reliability and the firm's internal efficiency stem from numerous contacts your client has with your firm. Actually understanding your client's objectives and instructions and then doing as you agreed, in every detail, is taken as a sign of your reliability and creates confidence. Keep your promises – do what you said you would do, when you said you would do it. If you have not done so, have the courage to tell your client – do not try to pull the wool over their eyes. Agreeing to bill at certain stages and then not sending the bill is perceived as being unreliable and inefficient. Clients like to feel that you are an internally efficient and effective firm – if you get it right internally, the chances are you will handle their matter well. This is where support systems come into play and enable you to give an efficient and reliable service. However, whatever systems or accreditations your office has in place or has achieved, their effectiveness is down to the attitudes of the people using them.

Showing clients that you value them

> If you've got the feeling from them that *you* are the most important person in their life at that moment you speak to them, that's when you know you're going to get the service you want.

All clients want to feel that they matter to you and your firm. Making a client feel valued often depends on small things and simply comes down to the way in which you treat them as people. Taking two minutes to greet the client in reception makes the client feel that at least they are starting off on a level playing field. You are familiar with the layout of your offices, but your client will not be and it creates additional stress for an already nervous client to have to seek you out in your office. Give the client your undivided attention in a clear and tidy room. Show that you are genuinely interested in the client's well-being. Do not keep clients waiting without a very valid reason – you are not the only busy person. Taking phone calls when a client is waiting in reception is not only annoying to a client, it suggests that another client's matter is of greater value to you.

> You've made all the effort to come and see them and then they keep you waiting for ten minutes whilst they're on the phone. Now they know you're coming . . . it's basically telling you that your time is not important.

Clients should always perceive that their instructions are important to you and that you are really working on their behalf.

> I was in a contract race. The solicitor was really helpful . . . He was always there to sign things and speed things up to get the house. That is why we keep using him.

As soon as I rang it prompted them. The letter was in the post or the solicitor had made the telephone call that day, but not if I did not ring.

Making a client feel valued is the converse of being complacent in respect of a client's instructions. Clients should never have the impression that their matter has been put 'on the back burner', a situation that can occur at the end of a litigation file when all the work has been done save the recovery of costs from the other side, for example. To a fee earner, the matter is virtually over and of little interest. The client, however, is still waiting for his or her money. Psychologically, the matter is most definitely not over and the client still wants the same effort expended in the collection of the money.

A major cause of clients feeling undervalued arises when they feel that they have been passed from pillar to post. Several fee earners have handled their matter and, with each change, they have had to 'reinstruct' the new fee earner because he or she has not been fully briefed. Changing fee earners unexpectedly may be inevitable but there are ways of making sure that the client still feels his or her matter is to be valued by the firm. If a proper introduction to the new fee earner cannot be made, that person should introduce him or herself and explain the background to the change and should at the very least be familiar with the file.

A professional approach

Everyone is involved in delivering the service and all must be seen by clients to undertake their tasks reliably and efficiently and to have a professional approach to their work. Offices should have an aura of calm efficiency and it is up to a firm's partners to set standards and to ensure that staff understand their responsibilities. Be mindful of the impression that receptionist cover on a switchboard can create with clients. Lunchtimes can be a very busy period and an office junior without training can come across as extremely unprofessional and a poor reflection of your firm. Your reception and offices should look smart and professional and appropriate for the client market you are serving. However, do not concentrate on improving your offices, letter heading or the other tangible aspects of your service at the cost of the more important issues in the relationship if you are trying to improve client service.

Commercial clients: how commercially aware are you?

In addition to the above key elements of service performance, corporate and commercial clients derive real value if you give advice that is relevant and pertinent to their needs and that helps them progress their own business. The practicality and creativity of your advice are important determinants of their assessment of your technical abilities. It is essential that you know and understand your client's business and that there is sufficient trust in the relationship for you to feel able to give commercial, practical advice rather than advice that is couched purely in legal terms. You have to understand the main commercial parameters within which your clients operate and their objectives throughout a matter. Clients really value advice that is given in terms that mirror their own approach to problems.

> He does know what our business is about and the kind of things we're looking for in deals, the kind of way we like to structure deals, that does help.

> It goes back to putting things in context. It's not just legal advice, it's legal with a commercial undertone.

> . . . in terms of added value or value to the business or quality of service, their knowing about it or their knowing me and how I'm going to react – not so much about what I want to hear but how I want to hear it. It's that knowledge that gives you the value.

> Occasionally they haven't been flexible enough, in terms of taking a business decision, they are only advising on the law.

It may not be easy but you have to find a balance in the relationship between adopting a commercial attitude and your own inherent professionalism that can lead to perceptions of overcaution, of being 'too tied into the law', or of wanting to overnegotiate and overcomplicate issues. Clients also believe that some solicitors are too adversarial, even when the client perceives this to be against their interests.

> Lawyers seem to perceive problems differently don't they?

> The sort of minimalist response that says well the law says this and the law says that and if you do that you might be taking a risk but on the other hand. It's not a fat lot of help very often.

> Solicitors can get in a loop where they're actually conducting a personal professional argument on a point of law.

> It's the nature of the way they tend to approach these things that they tend magically to create confrontation.

Remember the different perspectives from which solicitor and client approach the relationship. You may think your advice is commercial, practical and relevant, but you are not the recipient of that advice. Keep checking with your client not only how you are doing but also what they think of the way any other fee earner with whom the client has contact gives advice. Clients will view your enquiries positively.

CHAPTER SUMMARY

1. Partners and managers *must* understand the roles that confidence and trust play in the client evaluation process. It forms an integral part of the solicitor–client relationship and should be stressed to *all* members of a firm.

2. Managers should monitor and measure a firm's service to ensure that it meets client expectations on the key performance areas.

3. Managers must understand the key performance areas for each of their client markets.

4. For commercial clients, partners and managers should ensure that all fee earners are aware of the impact of the delivery of advice in terms that are commercially relevant to the client. When recruiting, they should not only consider technical competence of the candidates but the ability to demonstrate commercial acumen.

5. Managers should appreciate the potential to differentiate their services for commercial clients on the basis of their fee earners' commercial acumen.

6. Training, training, training.

7. Partners leading by example.

Note

1   H. M. Stewart (1999), 'The evaluation of legal services by commercial and corporate clients – implications for service design and delivery', Ph.D. thesis, University of Bradford.

5

Creating value for money

- Clients' assessments of value for money are separate from those made in respect of their perceptions of confidence and value in the solicitor–client relationship
- Issues that impact on clients' assessments of value for money
- The importance of practical and relevant advice for commercial clients
- Hourly rates do not equate to value for clients

Perceptions of value for money

The fees you charge form the second strand in clients' assessments of value – whether they believe they are receiving value for money from your services. Clients view the financial arrangements quite independently of the relationship in which trust and confidence are developed and their existence in the relationship with your client does not lead to any decreased sensitivity to price. In fact, when it comes to your fees, clients regard you as they would any other contractor. They want to feel that the fee they pay is reasonable for the value they have gained from your service. However, although financial arrangements are assessed separately, if you mismanage them, you can destroy your client's confidence immediately. Therefore it is extremely important that they are handled to your client's satisfaction. Managing costs and the billing process is discussed in the next chapter. Here we look at what lies behind perceptions of value for money.

Clients have difficulties in assessing the value of legal services in monetary terms – what are they valuing? The true value of your service to clients has to reflect what *they* believe they have gained, and that is not based on your charge-out rate. The amount you charge and what your client thinks your service has been worth will not necessarily be the same. Even if your clients achieve their objectives, they may perceive that they have received poor service from you and consequently poor value and poor value for money. Lawyers provide legal services which, if they are delivered to your client's satisfaction, should provide you with a profit, but that does not come as of right.

Only if you have provided your clients with a service that has matched their expectations will they regard your bill as fair and representing good value. Otherwise, there will be a gap between what your recorded time suggests that you should be able to charge and what your client perceives as reasonable value, as shown in Figure 5.1. And those expectations are high – for a private client, the charge-out rate you quote per hour may be close to what they earn in a day.

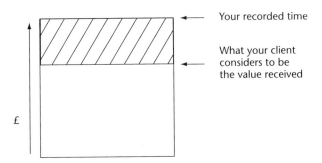

Figure 5.1   Perceptions of value received

Many private clients do not understand the numerous overheads involved in running a practice and you may need to explain some of these to them and that the charge-out rate does not represent your take-home pay. Commercial clients who often pay the higher rates of larger firms relate them to other costs and overheads, and to their own profit margins. Clients expect a high level of service for what it is costing them. The price you charge has to reflect what your client considers reasonable for the work done and its cost-effectiveness to the individual or the client's business.

Firms should remember not only that perceptions of value for money are subjective and will vary between clients but that they are also matter specific to individual clients. This is particularly relevant for commercial clients for whom a firm may have several ongoing matters at any one time. A strong relationship between a firm and client does not lead to decreased sensitivity to price. Clients evaluate value for each matter independently and they are not always willing to pay for a 'higher-quality' service. In a survey of its predominantly smaller company members by the Institute of Directors in 2000,[1] 50 per cent of the respondents considered that they were receiving poor value for money from their solicitors. The reasons given were that charge-out rates were too high, but also that work was charged at a uniform rate regardless of complexity. Firms should go out of their way to understand how the client perceives each situation. How important is the matter or type of matter to them? How do they perceive the risk? Take, for example, the same fee earner and client but two matters, one of which the client considers to be important and potentially carrying a high level of risk and one that is of a more routine nature. If the client is charged at the same rate on both matters, they will not perceive good value for money in respect of the routine work. This need only happen a couple of times and the client will begin to feel that they are being taken for granted and that the firm is becoming complacent regarding their instructions.

> While they were quite good they were getting very expensive so we changed.

> If you feel you are giving them good volumes of work then suddenly you feel that you are being taken advantage of on the relatively easy stuff.

Routine work should be undertaken at a lower charge-out rate wherever possible. This is easier in larger firms with a greater range of expertise, but still requires tactful handling if the work is to be undertaken by a more junior fee earner by emphasising that the client will receive better value. It can be more difficult in a smaller firm where an individual fee earner undertakes all the work for a client. Here, the fee earner may have to modify the charge-out rate after negotiation with the client and, if need be, increase it on the work that is perceived to be of greater value by the client.

You must not only understand whether your clients will consider your charges to be cost-effective for them, but also manage their expectations to let them know what to expect from your service. It is vital that you communicate with your clients so that they understand the value of what you are doing for them and they consequently consider they are receiving a service that provides value in terms of both confidence and price.

What impacts on perceived value for money?

Three issues have the principal impact on all clients' perceptions of value for money and a fourth also has a strong impact on the evaluation made by commercial clients:

(a) the level of perceived risk that the client is facing and the commensurate perceived level of technical expertise, experience, degree of ingenuity and creativity they believe they require;
(b) whether you conduct the matter to the client's satisfaction;
(c) whether you manage financial arrangements and the billing process to the client's satisfaction;

(d) the commercial acumen that you demonstrate when giving your advice and managing how the matter is conducted. They want to consider they are receiving 'good advice at a cost-effective price'.

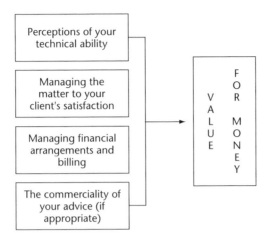

Figure 5.2   Creating perceptions of value for money

Risk and technical competence

Your technical skills are understandably taken into account when a client selects a fee earner or a firm for its perceived competence in an area of specialisation. Technical competence, experience, and sound judge-ment are seen to add value where clients consider their level of perceived risk warrants a higher charge-out rate. Work becomes increasingly price sensitive the more routine it is perceived to be. It is everyone's ambition to develop a niche and to charge a premium price, but, unfortunately, the markets for many legal services are now saturated. The low level of pub-lic funding for legal services also reduces price, irrespective of the client's perception of risk. Chapter 9 discusses designing profitable services that are price sensitive.

Many clients consider that, if the advice is good, it is money well spent. Fee earners who positively assist in enabling clients to achieve their objectives will be seen as providing good value for money.

> Richard's rates were £350.00 but that was a most impressive man who had this superb ability to pick up the threads of a very jumbled set of arguments and pull them together and play them back to you in a very logical way. So even writing a contract for us he was actually helping us sort out our logic in terms of presenting a case.

Similarly, fee earners who take the trouble to gain a thorough background knowledge of the subject matter will be seen as giving good value for money; visiting the scene of an accident, for example or viewing commercial premises so that only strictly relevant points are raised.

Commercial clients often look for a depth of expertise within specialist areas for risk avoidance and larger firms often gain because, although they are seen as more expensive, clients are usually prepared to pay their higher rates to obtain this.

Handling the matter to the client's satisfaction

Remember that clients are usually unfamiliar with legal processes – they will be unaware of a lot of the work that you have done to bring their matter to a conclusion, unless you have told them and involved them in achieving the result. Letting a client know what is happening throughout a matter serves both to manage their expectations and to communicate the value of your service to them. Failing to involve clients and allowing a misunderstanding to arise as to why their matter is taking a certain course can have a negative impact on perceptions of value for money. Clients want to feel an element of control and to be involved in the decision-making process. If your clients either do not understand or do not agree to a particular course, they will not unnaturally think they are getting a raw deal. You may be acting in the client's best interests, but if you have not explained the reasoning behind your judgement and agreed how the matter is to be handled with your client, the client may perceive that you are merely running a legal argument to score points against another solicitor – thereby increasing costs but not the benefit to the client. Clients speak of feeling that they have no control over the way in which they perceive that costs escalate and that they feel that they are being 'ripped off'.

Sometimes clients think handling a matter in an aggressive way against the other side is not always the most effective method of achieving a desired result, even in litigation. Others consider that this demonstrates your effort on their behalf. You have to discuss and agree the strategy with each client.

> It becomes a professional pride sort of thing, regardless of making the thing happen.

Clients want to feel that their matter is being handled as succinctly as possible, in terms of both timescale and the style of communication and documents. Unless they instruct you to the contrary, clients want their matter to progress as swiftly as possible in as economical a way as possible. Competence, workloads, levels of supervision, inclination, time management, available resources and internal systems all impact on a fee earner's ability to turn work around. Agreeing the means of communication at the outset will avoid a client feeling that the fee earner is trying to run up costs by 'overcommunicating'. Word processing and subsequently IT have resulted in the lengthening of documents, but clients do not perceive a corresponding increase in value for money. They do not see downloading a 'one size fits all' as good value – the content of all documents should be strictly relevant and, in general terms, the simpler and shorter, the better. 'The meter's running all the time' is a common phrase. It is up to a fee earner to ensure that the clients consider that they are receiving good value from that time.

Managing billing

We saw in Chapter 3 that clients approach our services with strong perceptions of risk about potential costs. Clients also have to trust a firm to be fair because there is often no tangible proof that work has actually been carried out. The way in which you explain costs to clients and discuss the method of billing with them has a serious impact on their perceptions of fairness for the price charged.

> It's nearly impossible to check because most of the work is not done in your presence.

Clients are reassured therefore when a firm is totally open about how it calculates its charges. This applies to both private and commercial clients except that the latter are likely to be more vociferous in their demands and want total transparency on billing and costs. Commercial clients in particular now demand a flexible approach to billing rather than just an hourly rate in which they bear all the risk. Following its study referred to earlier in this chapter, the Institute of Directors[2] recommends the remedy for concerns about high charges for straightforward work is to ensure greater transparency of charging structures. All clients want to know in advance how much a service is likely to cost, when and how frequently they will be billed, what their total indebtedness is to the firm at any one time and, when they receive a bill, they want to be able to understand how it is calculated. They do not want any shocks. In view of the adverse effect the poor handling of costs and billing can have on the overall relationship between solicitor and client, ways of establishing firm-wide billing protocols from setting up an initial agreement about costs with a client to their collection are discussed in Chapter 6.

The commerciality of your advice

We saw in Chapters 3 and 4 that commercial clients really value advice that is both practical and focused on their business needs. This demands that the fee earner has the requisite knowledge of a client's business and the markets within which it operates. Such knowledge and the tailoring of the manner in which advice is given to suit individual clients and the way in which they operate their business also has a strong influence on perceptions of value of money. Because of the dual impact that this factor has on both perceptions of value and value for money, firms should focus their marketing efforts on understanding how their commercial clients operate and discuss service levels with them at regular intervals. They should also ensure that non-partner fee earners share that understanding to ensure consistency of service. Although you may think that your advice is commercially relevant to your clients, you should always ask your clients for their opinion. Respondents to the Institute of Directors[3] survey said external lawyers often gave advice that was only 'by reference to the law without taking business realities into account' and that the advice was 'not definite enough'.

Value pricing

Billing habits in the past, in which clients have been unaware of the way in which bills have been calculated, are no longer acceptable. Clients, particularly commercial clients, are increasingly looking for alternatives to hourly rate billing from solicitors. They expect to be offered a fixed price whenever possible and if not, then an alternative form of billing that does not involve them bearing the full risk. Firms must take the initiative. Clients want clarity about costs. Discussing costs with clients at the outset and the respective cost–benefit of courses of action presents an invaluable opportunity to see how your clients perceive value and provides you with insight into the areas in which you need to manage your clients' expectations. Such discussions require careful thought – not only about how to achieve what your client wants but also with regard to the needs of the firm in terms of profitability and cash flow. This necessitates firms understanding the impact of various methods of billing on their cash flow and profitability and the requisite financial management involved is discussed in Chapter 12. Many firms are reluctant to consider anything other than hourly rate billing but, in addition to giving current clients the service they want, innovative pricing structures and packages can be a useful marketing aid. Try discussing them with a client with whom you have a good relationship and allow the client to choose which method they prefer.

We have already seen that some services are price sensitive. Firms should not be afraid to offer different rates to clients according to the client's perceived level of risk, with commensurate variation in fee-earner level if appropriate. In some cases, the same fee earner may have to undertake work at different rates for the same client, providing that the client is willing to pay a higher figure for the non-routine, higher-risk work. Firms should also be prepared to offer differing rates to different client markets, according to the perceived risk and price sensitivity of the work. What counts is the profitability of fee income. These issues and the financial management information that you need to manage your profitability are discussed more fully in Chapters 9 and 12.

CHAPTER SUMMARY

1. Managers should be aware of the independent role of cost-effectiveness in a client's overall assessment of value.

2. Managers should understand that charge-out rates do not equate to perceptions of value for money to clients. Clients' expectations that they should be offered a method of billing that shares some of the risk are increasing.

3. Managers should be aware of the areas of service that impact on perceptions of value for money, in particular the way a firm handles costs and billing with clients.

4. The reason that commercial clients leave a firm often comes down to a lack of understanding on the part of the firm of what the client perceives as value for money in any matter.

5. Fee earners need training to ensure they appreciate the adverse effect that failing to involve a client has on perceptions of value for money.

6. Have the courage to discuss alternative methods of billing with clients.

7. Managers should understand the profitability of work and the margins on it using different methods of billing (see Chapter 12).

Notes

1   S. Allen, 'Companies rap "high rates"' [2000] *Gazette*, 15 December.
2   Ibid.
3   Ibid.

Managing billing

KEY POINTS _____

- It is essential to manage the billing process to clients' satisfaction
- Clients are concerned about costs. They need information not only at the beginning but throughout a matter
- Alternative forms of billing; some pros and cons for the client and the firm
- Sending bills

Firm–client relationships

Communicating the value of your efforts to clients and managing costs and billing to manage their expectations should enable you to maximise billing potential, reduce aged debt and disbursement levels and give the desired level of profit sought by partners. We saw in the last chapter that the way in which firms manage billing has a strong impact on perceived value for money but few firms manage costs and billing well. Almost all firms will have clients who are not satisfied with the way in which this process has been handled, whatever the size of firm, level of expertise and however well the firm provides the rest of its service.

Clients view the relationship they have with a firm in respect of costs and financial arrangements quite distinctly from the relationship they have with an individual fee earner involving trust and confidence. Unfortunately, mismanaging the former can undo all your efforts in respect of the latter. This aspect of your service is therefore so important that every firm should have a billing protocol by which *all* its members must abide, without exception. It is not possible to dictate how a fee earner conducts a relationship with a client because such relationships involve interactions between people. However, rules can be laid down about billing procedures because they are in clients' interests.

All clients, private and commercial, approach legal services with concern about the total cost of the service and the unpredictability of it. They view hourly rate billing as 'the meter's running all the time'. Seen from the clients' viewpoint, unless they are offered a fixed price, the contract on costs seems totally open ended and at their risk. They do not know what could or should happen and often feel a situation is largely beyond their control. They want as much information about costs at the outset as it is possible for the solicitor to give. The Solicitors' Costs Information and Client Care Code 1999 (the 'Code') was drawn up to ensure that firms address these needs and sets out the current information that firms must give to clients.

Communication at the outset

Discussing costs should be seen as an opportunity to come to an agreement that is satisfactory to both parties. Involving clients in the billing process alleviates some of their greatest concerns about your service. Working out the way in which the client is to pay to suit both the needs of the client and those of the firm for working capital and cash flow is a vital first step in the relationship. Although cynics claim that all clients are reluctant to pay, the majority want to know how much your service will cost and when they will have to pay, so they can budget accordingly. Is it not better for the client to decide that they cannot afford your services than for you to have to chase and probably ultimately write off the costs? It is a question of getting the balance right between the needs of the firm for cash flow and a fair return for time and effort expended and those of the client in terms of perceived value for money.

You should agree with your client how costs are to be assessed and when they are to be paid. If you meet with price resistance, emphasise the value of what you will give to them, not in technical terms but in the way in which you will handle the matter to meet their needs. It is rarely worth lowering your price because invariably that client will be dissatisfied with whatever you do for them. With an existing client, always check on past payment history; with a new client, do a credit check at the outset.

Involving the client at the outset in agreeing payment terms that

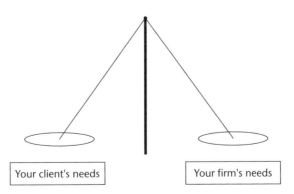

Figure 6.1   Getting the balance right

suit both the client's needs and those of the firm should lead to less payment resistance, although there will always be some clients who are reluctant to pay. Issues must not be fudged, but dealt with clearly and in unambiguous terms, including when legal services funding comes into operation, and its full implications, VAT and items such as letters in, phone calls, photocopying. Let clients know which fee earners will be involved and what their hourly rates are. You should discuss with your clients how you propose to deal with the issues in their matter and whether the potential benefit to them justifies the cost – doing such a cost–benefit analysis will allow your clients to assess whether it is worth their while proceeding. It is better not to begin the work than to find out half-way through that your client does not have the means to pay you. If you are offering a fixed price or giving an estimate up to a certain stage, be precise as to the terms of reference of the work that is included in that price. If you cannot give a firm estimate, give one within a range of figures.

Use your computer to flag up when costs have almost reached the amount of an estimate or fixed price and notify your client immediately in writing; then carry out a further cost–benefit analysis with the client. Talk to your client about alternative ways of proceeding, consider what the client wants out of the matter and then get the client's agreement to the course you advise to achieve those objectives. Let the client have a good estimate for the next stage of the work. Failing to do so not only puts the collection of further costs in jeopardy, but your client will view your omission as a sign of inefficiency, however well you are handling the technical aspect of the client's work. If you cannot give reliable estimates, nevertheless you must continue to give your client the best information possible.

Clients must be told which disbursements will be payable (although they should not necessarily be referred to as such) and when they will be due. A few firms are still poor at collecting in disbursements before they are paid out and their cash flow and working capital suffer accordingly. Some commercial practitioners are reluctant to collect in disbursements before the end of a matter for fear of upsetting clients. Ask yourself, would your client be so lenient with you if the roles were reversed? If you do not want to ask your commercial client to pay in advance, send a disbursements-only bill as soon as any have been paid out.

Communication during a matter

Communication about costs should take place not only at the beginning of a matter but throughout. The Code states that you must continue to update your client on costs. Clients will not always ask you for the information, therefore you must proffer it – in language and clear terms that they can understand. Bring the subject up regularly – it is not taboo. There must be no ambiguity. Try to put yourself in your client's shoes and see whether you would interpret what you are saying in a different way. It is worthwhile asking a colleague to check the clarity of a letter about costs: you know what you mean but, remember, it is alien territory for the client. If you send a series of letters about costs, ensure that they are consistent and present a short summary of previous information. Remember to notify your client of any changes in hourly rates, when a trainee qualifies for example, or the different rates for anyone else involved in the work. Do not assume that clients will realise that costs are mounting, even if they are aware of the work you are doing for them. You must always inform them on a regular basis, at least every six months according to the Code, but in reality on a far more frequent basis if costs are accumulating quickly. Where you can only bill on the conclusion of a lengthy matter, send clients regular statements of accrued costs. Discuss the regularity of these with the client at the outset. Some firms already allow their commercial clients online access to their own office account ledger balance.

Large commercial clients dictate the way in which the service is to be given and have specific requirements on billing, but smaller commercial clients do not always fare so well. Practitioners usually argue that clients do not want to be bothered discussing costs and billing processes at the beginning of each matter – they know and understand their clients, having acted for them for several years. Ask whether they have ever asked the clients whether they are satisfied with the service they receive and the answer is invariably no. While it may be a waste of everyone's time to discuss costs on repetitive business, and the Code takes this into account, you should make a point of having at least an annual discussion with the client to discuss the service generally and costs in particular: whether the client is satisfied; are there any other ways in which the firm could manage billing to assist the client – timing, information on bills, electronic delivery, payment by BACS, an alternative type of billing, etc. Clients will be pleased to have the discussion as it demonstrates your interest in them and that you do not take their work for granted.

Interim billing, where appropriate, should be agreed whenever possible. For clients, it is much better not to have the weight of costs on their shoulders and little and often is far preferable. If you bill clients soon after you have done the work, they will remember what you have done and their perception of its value will be greater. For firms, interim billing is a great help for cash flow and obviates the need to purge-bill. Agree to bill on a time basis rather than when the matter has reached a significant stage – the latter will mean that a significant amount of costs will also have accrued. Agree monthly, quarterly, etc., and then stick to your agreement, even if only a small amount of time has been recorded.

Your client will be waiting for your bill and if you really do not think it worthwhile sending a bill, let the client know. Keep to your agreement.

However, bear in mind that if it is not possible to give a fixed price or at least a reliable estimate up to a point in the matter, client satisfaction is not wholly dependent on the method of billing. For many clients, giving them full information, in advance, about what, how, and when they will be billed and who will carry out the work is of greater importance. This information forms a sound foundation for the relationship, but then you must stick to the terms of your agreement with the client.

Confirming the agreement in writing

Solicitors commonly refer to a former Rule 15 letter as that which has to be sent to clients at the beginning of a matter containing the information they are required to give. Such letters are invariably extremely long-winded and difficult for even the most intelligent individual to comprehend. Try to read a letter from a client's point of view. Is it in simple, straightforward language? Is there any ambiguity? Although the Code provides that the information must be given in writing, it does not need to be in the form of a letter. Consider more creative ways of conveying the content. The firm's brochure for example, with inserts to tailor the information or an attractively laid-out document, professionally designed, with a lot of white space to make the content more digestible. If you feel more comfortable sending a letter, then ask several clients for their view on it and any ways in which it could be improved. Remember that the longer the letter, the less likely the client will either read it in full or understand the content.

- Keep paragraphs short.
- Use short sentences.
- Use bullet points for key points.
- Space the text so that it is approachable.

Whatever the format, your client should of course sign and return a duplicate of the agreement.

Alternative forms of billing

Computerised accounting systems put paid to the days when practitioners based their charges on the weight of a file. Hourly rate billing has many advantages for firms: it is relatively easy and efficient; helps with cash flow; allows a firm to know the value of its work in progress (WIP); is objective and a necessity in litigation and publicly funded work; and, above all, there is no risk to the firm. But it does nothing to alleviate the risk to clients nor does it always represent value to them. Led by commercial clients, all clients are now seeking alternative methods of billing in which the firm bears some of the risk. This poses not just a threat, but also a practical problem because, even if a firm's accountant, practice manager or cashier understands the cost of production and profitability of work, few of the partners or fee earners who discuss costs and billing methods with clients do. Firms should consider their organisational structures to ensure that the fee earner discussing cost with clients has full knowledge both of the alternatives that can be offered to the client and of the impact of each on the firm's profitability so that the needs of both firm and client will be met. Types of billing with suggestions for when they can be used and the comparative advantages and disadvantages for both firm and client are set out in Table 6.1. The financial management of some firms will need to step up a gear so that this knowledge is available. Chapter 12, on financial management, outlines issues that firms need to address to be aware of the implications of different types of billing on their cash flow and profitability.

Billing

The quid quo pro of making an agreement with your client must be that you get paid promptly and this has to be emphasised to your client at the outset as well. You should give details of your terms of payment, including interest if you intend to charge it. Never give a client an excuse for late payment – stick to your agreement. Send the bill when agreed, because your client will be waiting for it and will view its non-arrival as a sign of your inefficiency and unreliability. Being too busy or there being insufficient time recorded to warrant raising a bill is not an excuse. Let the client know why it has not been sent. Always send bills as soon as practically possible on the conclusion of a matter when your client can still remember the value of what you have done for them. Clients expect prompt delivery, they want to pay the bill and move on with their lives. Sending a bill three months later is not only an indication of inefficiency, it suggests that you are not concerned with being paid quickly. Billing protocols should include rules on the delivery of bills and billing should also be discussed in supervision meetings. All fee earners should understand client needs in relation to billing.

Books have been written about the format of bills that will delight clients and encourage them to pay instantly. Would that it were so simple. Most clients will be prepared to pay you if they think they have received good value in terms both of their trust and confidence in you and of perceived value for money. If you have discussed costs with your client at stages throughout the matter and involved them in the way it

Table 6.1 Comparisons of different methods of billing

Method of billing	When to use	Advantages for client	Disadvantages for client	Advantages for firm	Disadvantages for firm
Hourly rate	• When client wants it • When anticipated time cannot be foreseen with reasonable accuracy • Litigation where court assesses costs • Legal Services Commission funding	• Some clients like it • Can agree interim billing	• All risk on client • Does not necessarily correspond to perceived value	• Familiar • Easy • Firm takes none of risk • Helps in managing cash flow • Allows firm to justify all time spent if a dispute • Good cost-accounting tool • Can increase rates to pass on increased overheads	• Can encourage inefficiency in working practices • Penalises technological advances – greater productivity by using IT not reflected in charge-out rate • Limits potential earnings by placing ceiling on how much can be earned • Firms can become over-focused on fee income and on highest fee earners. Ignores issues such as client loyalty rates, profitability, collection rates, experience, ingenuity, creativity or efficiency • Does not serve to differentiate your firm – rates set by competition and firms go for the 'middle ground'

Fixed fee	• For routine services where possible to foresee normal course of the matter and you can define what will be included in the fee
	• When you can estimate
		• Client knows what paying up front
		• Firm takes the risk
			• Client less likely to feel able to switch firms if dissatisfied	• Clarifies client's expectations
				• Forces firm to be efficient
				• Overcomes buyer resistance
					• Unprofitable if:
					  Costs of providing service exceed estimated cost
					  Service not performed efficiently
					  No specific definition of

	When to use			Considerations / Need to
	both the time involved and the level of fee earner required • For commodity services in a highly competitive market • For volume work on a repetitive basis • When you are prepared to accept the risk of unprofitability if time taken exceeds the costed time		• Can increase prices year on year • Aids competitive differentiation and marketing • Should make firm aware of cost of defined work • Can be keyed to perceived value to client	what is included and unforeseen circumstances arise • Need to: define work to be undertaken be able to estimate costs accurately collect data to have knowledge about costs
Blended fixed fee and hourly rate	When client wants reassurance on costs up to certain point and can then determine whether worthwhile proceeding further	Greater initial control	May influence client to instruct	Same as for fixed fees and and hourly rates above
Composite hourly rate of all fee earners involved	When several fee earners will be involved and the work follows a typical pattern so input of each different level of expertise is known	• Same as hourly • Should be better price for client • Rates can be quoted, monitored and compared by client	Same as hourly Useful for marketing	• Appears simple but depends on knowing costs of production • Work must be delegated to appropriate level to ensure profitability • Delegated work will need adequate supervision to ensure quality • Firm will have to educate client to ensure client does not expect senior fee earner to do all work

Table 6.1 Comparisons of different methods of billing–*continued*

Method of billing	When to use	Advantages for client	Disadvantages for client	Advantages for firm	Disadvantages for firm
Percentage fee Constant or graduated	Where the total amount can be predetermined as in probate or conveyancing, some rights issues	Certainty for client Reflects amount involved Not time dependent	May be expensive for work involved	Easy to state to client May be highly profitable	• If set too high, may not be competitive • If set too low, may be unprofitable • If complications, firm will bear the risk
Conditional fee	In litigation after a careful assessment of the risks involved and an appropriate agreement of the success fee				• Firm bears all risk • Uneven cash flow • Cost of funding work is high
Contingent fees	• Depends on results achieved in non-contentious work – percentage of total • Non-litigious matters where there can be clear agreement as to what the desired results of the matter will be, whether positive, e.g. achieving a desired objective or negative, e.g. avoiding a liability • Terms of representation can be clearly defined • Use if want to represent	Client only pays if desired result achieved Client can be represented even if cannot otherwise afford to pay No risk to client		Can be highly profitable	• Firm bears all risk • Depends on results, not time taken • Uneven cash flow • Time and effort may exceed estimates

	client who would otherwise be unable to pay • Use for good-quality work with good chance of success		
Retainer	• If requested by client and the value of the fee is sufficiently profitable to cover the demands on fee earners' time • Work it relates to must be clearly defined • Should be set for an initial trial period during which use can be assessed and retainer reviewed • Should only be offered for relatively low-level work or general advice which will not be overly time consuming	Client knows spend on legal fees for specified work types	• May influence a client to give all work • Assists cash flow	• Need to consider time spent on previous work for client to make realistic assessment of amount to be paid • Need to keep careful records of time spent and matter types undertaken • Need to agree level of fee earner to undertake work • Need to review regularly • Clients may make greater demands of your time

has progressed, then when you send a bill that accords with the terms of your financial agreement, most clients will pay. The narrative should be sufficiently lengthy to communicate the value of work you have undertaken but not overlong and not in prosaic language. Above all, the bill should include a breakdown of the way it has been calculated. Unless you have previously agreed this format, 'To professional charges for advising you on . . . £950.00', is not enough. Omitting information about the calculation of the amount is a common failing and one that upsets clients. Give details of the hours worked and by whom and the appropriate rates, numbers of phone calls, etc. Include them in a schedule if you prefer. Some practitioners do not send these details initially, but on subsequent request from the client. However, that may be too late and you may have already upset your client by not providing the information in the first place. If you have any doubts, discuss it with the client beforehand. Contrary to what many practitioners believe, clients actually welcome such approaches because it demonstrates that you are concerned about meeting their expectations. When sending regular bills to a commercial client, ask them about the format and the details to be included to make their internal processing easier, and how many copies they would like.

There are circumstances in which you may have been waiting to receive instructions from a client for several months and want to send a bill in any event. Or you may feel that, regardless of the initial agreement, your client may baulk at the amount you would like to charge because:

- you have not stuck to the agreement, e.g. the time taken exceeds the estimate and you did not go back to your client to obtain an agreement to carry on;
- you have not given regular updates on accrued costs and your client will not equate the quoted hourly rate with the cost of the time the work has actually taken;
- the client may not consider that he or she has received value either in terms of having achieved anything substantive from the work or in relation to his or her perception of the firm's service.

Never send any bill that might surprise a client; always discuss it with them first. If you send clients a bill that they consider to arrive 'totally out of the blue and for five times more than anticipated', not only are you unlikely to get paid, you will also undo all your efforts in building relationships with those clients. Have courage and phone your client first. London commercial firm Campbell Hooper[1] found that 84 per cent of respondents to a survey of 40 companies ranging from blue chip to small businesses, preferred to discuss bills with lawyers before receiving them. Discussion provides an opportunity to remind clients of all the work that has been involved and to obtain their agreement as to the amount.

Clients maintain that this is an important step psychologically – when the bill arrives, they will be expecting it and you are likely to be paid reasonably quickly. If you do not make the phone call, the bill may be a shock to your client who will put it to the bottom of the pile where it will remain until you have the embarrassment of chasing it. You will also have a dissatisfied client whom you may not retain.

Discounting bills rarely has a positive influence on clients: '£950.00 but say £900.00', for example. Clients merely wonder why you have not just charged them £900.00 in the first place. Instead, contact the client in advance and agree the amount with the client, and then, as with all bills, send the bill promptly.

Some firms expect fee earners to hit monthly billing targets and there is a consequent rush to bill each month end. However, care must be taken to ensure that such bills accord with client agreements. Purge billing as the year end approaches, or to improve cash flow, should be avoided unless you take care not to upset clients. If you have entered into an agreement on costs with your client, and you have stuck to it by billing as you agreed, there should be no need either to have the 'purge' or to send a bill to your client at that time. The bill will not be anticipated and will be seen as outside the terms of the agreement.

Aged debt

Firms should also have a system for collecting bills, and again, one to which all members should adhere (see Chapter 12). The prompt and efficient collection of costs is the final impression that a client may have of your firm.

If a client does not pay within the time allowed, the first questions to ask should be:

- Has the bill actually been sent?
- Is the client dissatisfied with the way the matter has been handled?
- Does the client consider that he or she received poor value? If so, why?

If the latter, appropriate steps to deal with the client's grievance should be taken immediately. How to handle complaints is covered in Chapter 14.

Note

1   [2001] *Gazette*, 29 November.

7

The external perspective: what clients really think of you

KEY POINTS _____

- The importance of obtaining clients' views
- Management responsibilities must be allocated
- Overcoming objections to obtaining views
- Different ways of seeking clients' views
- Which methods for which clients?
- Practical points to consider when drafting survey questionnaires

Why find out?

Firms that analyse their client database invariably find that the majority of their revenue comes from the repeat instructions of existing clients or from new clients who have been recommended by them. Why then do firms spend time and money on trying to attract new clients rather than concentrating on looking after their existing ones? Demonstrating to clients that you really do care about them and value them as clients will invariably produce more work. Successful practices of all sizes serving all markets recognise the competitive differentiation they can achieve by proactively taking steps to match their service to meet client needs. You cannot assume that you know whether your client is happy with your service; failing to ask may be interpreted as complacency towards the client. Nor is it remotely unprofessional to ask a client whether your service could be improved in any way. So how do firms set about obtaining clients' views of their service?

A client relationship management programme

A client relationship management programme means a formal framework to support a firm's efforts to develop relationships within its selected client markets. A significant part of such a programme relates to obtaining clients' views of current service levels, deciding on the remedial steps to be taken and actually implementing those steps. Some form of management structure in which responsibilities are allocated is essential to overcome potential apathy and/or resistance and to ensure action is taken and sustained. The size of the client relationship management framework will depend upon the size and type of practice. In a smaller firm, responsibility will probably lie with one partner who has the support of other partners, whereas in larger firms the framework will probably comprise at least one partner supported by other managerial or administrative staff and possibly representatives from the various departments within the firm. The success of such a programme will be dependent on the culture of the firm and the motivation of partners, fee earners and staff to embrace client service and to take on board the need to change behaviours if that will serve to enhance client perceptions of the service. It will have to be backed up by a willingness to introduce and adhere to new systems and procedures to ensure a consistently reliable and efficient service for clients. Obtaining clients' views without a willingness to change will be a waste of resources. In this chapter, we look at ways of gaining a greater understanding of what clients want from our services; Chapter 8 deals with implementing changes.

Overcoming objections

One of the biggest stumbling blocks to obtaining clients' views is likely to be your fellow partners. Solicitors are not generally used to getting feedback on how they are doing, although this is changing with the increasing use of partner appraisals. Many feel threatened by the prospect and cannot understand the need to seek clients' views. Getting feedback from clients should always be seen as a positive step, a means of improving service levels and of remaining competitive. Understanding what your clients want from your service can suggest areas for change or innovation to provide you with a leading competitive edge. We live in a consumerist society and clients expect to be asked for their views and for those views to be taken into account. Failing to talk to clients leads to perceptions of complacency and a consequent reduction in market share. Some of the reasons likely to be proffered with counter-arguments are set out in Table 7.1.

The pros and cons of various methods of obtaining clients' views

Many solicitors believe that they understand what their clients want from their service and that they provide them that desired level of service. It

Table 7.1 Common objections to seeking clients' views

Common objections to asking clients for their views	Ideas for gaining commitment
Cannot trouble clients	Clients do not object – they are more likely to feel flattered if you explain why you are conducting your survey. You will only upset them if, having asked for their views, you do not listen to them and take any requisite remedial action. By using the information to improve your service or understand where expectations need to be managed, you can plan your service to meet their expectations. This in the longer term will lead to an improvement in the firm's image and to better-quality work
	Failure to obtain clients' views may mean that you are unaware of the potential for client dissatisfaction. Not only are you likely to lose clients but, in the meantime, they may be damaging your reputation. Commercial clients may consider that you are complacent towards them if you do not ask about service levels
It will unsettle the relationship with the client, 'my client'	Emphasise the long-term benefits and the potential cost of not doing so. Ask clients their views on other partners and then use their favourable responses as a persuasion tool
Clients' expectations will only be raised	If you do not find out from clients what their expectations are, how are you going to find out which need to be managed? Some clients do have expectations that you cannot meet, but by explaining your reasons at the outset, clients will not be disappointed
	Emphasise that feedback will be given to clients
Only dissatisfied clients will respond	Not necessarily the case, but, in any event, it is their views that you probably need to know
Clients will use it as an excuse to push down fees	If you operate in a client market in which price is the paramount issue, you can plan your service to enable you to deliver a low-cost service either by the effective use of IT or by using well-trained and well-supervised junior fee earners. Clients cannot expect to have a partner dealing with a matter at a rock-bottom price. You can begin to communicate the value of your service to your clients to ensure that they do consider they are receiving value for money

Table 7.1   Common objections to seeking clients' views – *continued*

Common objections to asking clients for their views	Ideas for gaining commitment
It implies to clients that there is a problem	Always explain your motives to clients and approach any survey as a means of improving what is probably already good Emphasise that feedback will be given to clients
Fee earners do not want to recognise the problems or do not like the prospect of criticism or of potential failure	Lead by example, particularly the senior partner or other willing partners. Junior partners may be more open to the idea. Approach any client survey in an open way. Fully communicate the reasons for carrying it out and how the results will be used to everyone in the firm before you go ahead Always deal with issues that arise in a very positive and sensitive manner – learn by mistakes
We did not enter the profession to become salespeople	Clients will only perceive it as a selling exercise if you treat it as one. Do not try to cross-sell your services when trying to get their views on your service performance
It is unprofessional	Clients are used to giving their views about almost every other service and usually welcome a firm's efforts to improve its service. Clients may have to obtain customers' opinions about their own industry/service. Accountants have sought their clients' views for several years. Get your clients to endorse your efforts
Too busy	Emphasise the long-term benefits of conducting the survey
What are we going to do with the information?	Analyse it and identify from the results how you can improve your service. Does anyone need specific training? Does everyone need general training on client service? Do you need to improve your office systems and procedures? Do you need to manage client expectations if they are unrealistic? Use appraisals to monitor performance. Links can also be made to remuneration packages Ensure that you take client service into account when recruiting and when inducting new members into the firm

may be presumptuous to hold such an opinion about any client, because perceived complacency towards a relationship with a client is one of the primary major reasons that clients leave firms. The different perspectives from which solicitor and client approach their relationship mean that solicitors cannot accurately judge what their clients think of their service. In addition, there can be considerable inconsistency in client perceptions of a firm's service, across partners and fee earners. Even where clients consider that some fee earners give an excellent service, the service from others may fall far short of meeting clients' expectations. In view of the importance of meeting the needs of your chosen client markets in developing your practice, it is essential that you fully understand what they are. Seeking clients' views of your service and ways in which it could be improved should be your prime marketing objective.

A considerable number of practices profess to have client satisfaction as a main organisational goal, but the majority of these do so from a reactive stance. They respond to deficiencies in client service once they have been detected, but that may be too late and may result in at worst the loss of the client and at best write-offs of costs or WIP. The dissatisfaction will also have involved time and stress for the fee earner involved in resolving the issue. A lot of firms seek feedback from clients in satisfaction surveys that are routinely sent out on the conclusion of a matter, again from a reactive stance. The questionnaires are usually in a standard format, designed in-house, and contain questions that rarely relate to the issues that are most important to the particular client market. Although having phone calls answered promptly by a receptionist is important, the firm's management should ensure that this happens without having to ask a client for the information. Questions that relate to attitudes and behaviours are rarely asked; whether the client always felt that the fee earner involved them in what was happening, for example, or listened to what they wanted from a situation, or kept them informed or communicated with them satisfactorily so they understood the reasons for not being able to achieve their objectives. Questions that relate to costs and the management of billing are posed even less frequently. Response rates are often poor because the client considers it to be just another routine survey that is not worth their time completing. Although some managers may analyse the responses periodically and instigate improvements in processes and procedures, the information gained is of little benefit because it does not relate to issues that clients really care about.

Proactive firms on the other hand, try to identify what is important to the clients they serve and then to ask the *right* questions, ones that do matter to clients. The best way to do this is to allow clients in each market to develop the questions themselves, either through a series of carefully prepared and handled client interviews, or by focus groups. The latter are not commonly used within the legal profession but practitioners who have run them in conjunction with an external agency report that they have proved a particularly effective means of establishing the important issues to clients of a particular market. They are outlined with other methods of surveying clients in Table 7.2.

However, how you obtain clients' views will depend upon your resources, the work type, nature of clients and the clients' value to the firm. Various methods are given below. Limited resources should not be a reason for not carrying out the exercise, although sometimes you have to be creative. An immigration lawyer, for example, asks clients at about six-month intervals, during normal office attendances, whether there is any way in which service could be improved. Notes are taken, kept in a separate pocket in the file and periodically collated with notes from other files. Any required action is then decided upon and implemented. A sole practitioner doing commercial work (with relatively few clients) sent a questionnaire with a Christmas card and the promise of bottle of wine if they responded. He reported the information that he received back was extremely useful, not only in respect of service levels, but also with information about which other legal services his clients wanted him to provide.

Whichever method you select, it is important to think about how you are going to collate information received, and to use it to improve service levels. Personal interviews are fine but if the interviewer is also the person handling the matter and is told anything adverse, they are unlikely to disclose the information. If the problem relates to the fee earner's attitude or behaviour, that fee earner may not know what to do to improve. The advantages and disadvantages of several methods of surveying clients are set out in Table 7.2.

Table 7.2   Different ways of obtaining clients' views

Method	Pros	Cons
Postal survey: one-off	Useful for benchmarking	Questions have to be tailored to the specific client market to obtain full, meaningful information
	Provides comprehensive way of obtaining views of a large sample of clients	
	Best way to reach clients whose responses might be biased or distorted in a personal interview	To maintain credibility with clients and firm, have to put improvements into effect
		Cost of preparing, sending and analysis
		Poorer response rate than other methods but this can be improved by using an independent third party
		Slower than other methods

Table 7.2 Different ways of obtaining clients' views – *continued*

Method	Pros	Cons
Postal survey: after every transaction	Monitors clients' views on an ongoing basis	Similar to one-off survey
		Need to ensure that results are not ignored. Have to ensure that they do not fall into disrepute, either from fee earners' or clients' viewpoints
		As for one-off postal surveys
Telephone surveys	Gathers information quickly	Time consuming
	Allows the interviewer to clarify questions	Interviews have to be short and are not too personal
	Higher response rate than postal survey	Clients may not like being 'put on the spot' although a prior call may be made to arrange a convenient time
Personal interviews by: lead 'relationship' partner review partner or marketing executive/external consultant	The most versatile method	Have to ensure interviewer asks questions about issues important to the client. Will client express honest and open views to the person who has been handling the file? Will that person handle the interview in an unbiased and undistorted way?
	Interviewer can ask more questions and, in an unstructured interview, more probing questions	
	Useful for key clients	Will independent interviewer have sufficient knowledge of the work type or the firm?
	Can be used by firms with limited resources, by fee earner as a matter progresses	
		Most time-consuming method
		Needs more administration and planning
		Information has to be analysed and collated to obtain benefits
		Good opportunity to explore clients' needs more fully and to see what other work the firm can do – can yield good results in the form of additional work and therefore, although most expensive method, can be cost-effective

Table 7.2   Different ways of obtaining clients' views – *continued*

Method	Pros	Cons
Focus groups of 8–10 clients from a single client market. About 90 min. duration After an initial focus group, subsequent groups need only be held every few years to ensure that the needs of the market have not changed. Other means of obtaining clients' views can be used, e.g. a postal or phone survey	Better to ask clients to attend 'blind' so they believe they are to discuss legal service in general and not of your specific firm. Very useful way of establishing aspects of service important to that market. You will still be able to identify where their expectations are not being met Often much fuller, more meaningful information because clients spark views off each other Clients usually willing to attend if given small payment or gift	Needs careful planning, an independent and experienced moderator, and an independent venue Even after transcription by moderator, you may have to analyse responses and identify what action needs to be taken

Which method for which clients?

In addition to your resources, how you obtain clients' views will depend upon your client markets and the different segments you serve. You may decide to take a snapshot view by conducting a one-off survey of all your clients, or of all your commercial or private clients, against which you can benchmark in the future. If so, you must tailor the questionnaires to ensure that you ask appropriate questions of each market. Otherwise, base your selection according to client market or segment and the value of the client to the firm in terms of volume of work and/or profitability. Your financial management information should ensure that you have information on client profitability. Divide your clients according to the percentage of turnover and the profitability of each. Figure 7.1 gives one means of segmenting clients.

High-value, key clients

These are usually commercial and with a strong, profitable relationship with the firm. Even though you may discuss service on a regular basis, it is still useful, and usually appreciated by the client, if you have an annual interview devoted entirely to improving service delivery. These interviews are often conducted by either by a lead partner or the firm's managing partner, and can be structured or unstructured, depending on the client.

Figure 7.1 Segmenting clients

In either case, it is essential to have carried out thorough preparation beforehand to ensure that you are as aware as possible about all aspects of the client's work. In a structured interview, make sure that you ask questions about issues that will be important to the client. In addition to the functional aspects of the relationship, questions dealing with the 'softer' issues should also be asked – any breakdown in confidence, lack of personal chemistry between fee earner and client, for example. Take the opportunity to visit your client's business and to understand more about it. Do not give a sales pitch, but listen to what the client tells you – opportunities for additional work should become apparent.

Key clients

These may be commercial or private client. With commercial clients, there may be relationships that you wish to nurture and encourage in which case you may decide to carry out an interview as with a high-value key client. Similarly, if the client instructs several fee earners, it may be useful for a relationship partner to discuss service levels regularly with the client. Alternatively, you can use a one-off postal survey to monitor perceptions of service levels.

With a private client who provides a lot of work, you can discuss service issues with the client on a regular basis, either in a specific interview or at stages during a matter. Private clients may be more reluctant or shyer to inform you of any problems and a one-off postal survey often provides useful information.

General clients

Use a one-off postal survey or focus groups of members of the client market. In addition, clients always appreciate being asked during a matter whether they think, for example, that communication is working well between you or whether they understand all aspects of costs. If you only raise the subject at the end of the matter, you miss the opportunity to rectify any perceived problems en route, and the possibility of repeat business or recommendations.

High-volume, low-value clients

Use a postal survey at the end of a matter or focus groups of members of the client market. It is always useful for a supervisor to carry out spot-check interviews of clients to receive current feedback on service levels in a telephone survey for instance. This information is useful in establishing what is important to clients so that the questionnaire can be completely relevant to the client market.

Drafting client survey questionnaires: some points to consider

So what?

What are you trying to achieve? You must always have a clear objective when you are designing a survey questionnaire. For example if you want to learn and understand your firm's image in the marketplace, ask some of your professional contacts who refer work as well as some of your clients. You can often do this informally. Be aware, though, that if you want clients' views of your service you have to ask your clients – there is no substitute, although professional contacts can add some useful points. The questions you ask of clients have to reflect the aspects of your service that are important to them. Merely asking whether your client is satisfied with your service does not tell you how to improve it.

Clients are more likely to give truthful answers if their responses are anonymous, but you can either include a question asking the client to specify which departments in the firm they have used or use some means of identifying the department sending the questionnaire, a code for example. It will be helpful to identify whether any perceived shortfall of service is unique to any department or is endemic across the firm. Send the survey by first-class post with a letter explaining its purpose and a stamped addressed reply envelope. It is useful to specify the date by which you would like responses to be returned. Response rates are some-times improved if the replies are returned to an independent third party for analysis and clients may also feel freer to express their views. Response rates of up to 50 per cent can be obtained in these circumstances.

Your sample

You should decide how many clients you are going to survey and whether they are to come from a cross-section of your firm or by department. Do not let fee earners interfere with the selection. You want to know all views from clients, good and bad. The poor responses should be viewed positively as a means of identifying where you can improve. Statistically, you should have at least 30 responses before you can begin to consider that you have a representative sample of your clients. It is not unreasonable to expect a response rate of 25 per cent for a one-off survey, but, the more clients in the sample, the better. Many firms report poor response rates to questionnaires sent out at the end of each matter. One explanation may be that they are similar to 'hotel bedroom'-type surveys with little content that is important to the client.

Your questionnaire

The introduction

Explain the aim of the survey and tell clients how to complete the questionnaire in a brief introduction.

The questions

Use closed questions if you are using a rating scale. Concentrate on issues that are most important to clients – those that relate to the service given by fee earners. Clients are more concerned as to whether the fee earner returned a phone call than whether the phone was answered promptly by the receptionist. A survey of commercial/corporate clients will need additional questions to those on a survey for private client markets. Keep the format simple and uncluttered. Customise the wording of the questions for the client market. Check with a few clients that you have covered all the important aspects of service and that the questionnaire is user friendly before you send it out. Some general questions follow – the wording may need amendment or additional questions may be required to ensure that they are relevant to your client market.

1. *The work we undertake for you is carried out in the agreed timescale?*
2. *We give you the right amount of information about your matter in a timely way?*
3. *We give full attention and priority to your matter?*
4. *We always respond promptly to your messages?*
5. *Your solicitor is always available when you need him/her?*
6. *We always listen to you and understand your concerns?*
7. *We understand your objectives in the matter and always work towards achieving them?*
8. *We take account of how you want the matter to proceed?*
9. *We give advice in clear, simple terms?*
10. *Our letters and documents are clear and concise?*

11. *Everyone in the firm demonstrates a professional approach to you?*
12. *You are always made to feel a valued and important client?*
13. *We discuss the basis of our charging with you at the beginning of the matter?*
14. *We agree with you at the outset how and when the matter is to be billed?*
15. *We discuss costs with you regularly throughout the matter?*
16. *Our bills are always in accordance with our agreement?*
17. *Our bills are presented in such a way that you can understand how they are calculated?*
18. *We are cost conscious in handling your work?*

In addition, commercial clients should be asked their opinions on the commercial acumen you demonstrate in giving advice. Some additional questions to reflect this and the ongoing nature of the relationship are as follows:

1. *We demonstrate commercial awareness when advising you?*
2. *We are aware of the commercial parameters within which you have to operate?*
3. *We fully understand your aims and objectives in each matter?*
4. *We present practical solutions to your problems?*
5. *We understand your approach to problems and advise you accordingly?*
6. *Your matters are appropriately staffed to provide you with a cost-effective service?*
7. *We are willing to meet you at your place of business?*
8. *We offer proactive advice in a manner that fits your needs?*
9. *We keep you informed of the full range of our services?*
10. *We give you information on points of contact within the firm for our different services?*
11. *You are able to discuss any breakdown in trust or confidence in any aspect of our services with a partner?*
12. *We are flexible in our approach to billing?*
13. *Our services are cost-effective for the value gained?*

The scales

Research has indicated that survey respondents may use the mid-value in a rating scale with odd numbers to record a 'don't know' or ambivalent response. The problem with a 1 to 4 scale is that it does not always allow sufficient variation for clients to express their views. One alternative is to give a descriptor to each value on a 1 to 5 or 1 to 7 scale. For example, the following scales can be placed alongside each question and clients asked to tick or circle the number that most accurately represents their view.

Performance 5-point rating scale with descriptors

Excellent	Very good	Good	Needs improvement	Unsatisfactory
5	4	3	2	1

Another way is to provide additional values around the mid-value so that the respondents have to think about their response to the question.

Performance 5-point rating scale with descriptors and additional mid-point values

Excellent	Very good	Good			Needs improvement	Unsatisfactory
5	4	3+	3	3–	2	1

Measuring importance

If you want to know how important each aspect of service is to clients, you can add another scale such as the one below, again alongside each question. This gathers information that allows you to address any issues that are particularly important to clients where your service does not meet their expectations.

Importance 5-point rating scale

Extremely important	Very important	Important	Not very important	Unimportant
5	4	3	2	1

Some additional questions

You can also ask for views on the overall impression of the quality of service offered by a firm. The responses are a useful general indicator, but greater reliance should be placed on the responses to other specific questions. You learn nothing from being told that your performance is satisfactory – what you need to know is how can it be improved. How could you make it excellent? The following is an example of an overall rating scale. Once again, the mid-point value could be expanded (see above).

Responses to additional questions often throw light on those to closed questions with rating scales and can suggest ways in which the level of service can be improved. In addition to some of a general nature,

Overall rating scale

Please consider your overall impression of the quality of service offered by [name firm] and then circle the number that most accurately represents your view.

Excellent	Very good	Good	Needs improvement	Unsatisfactory
5	4	3	2	1

you can pose questions to give you information on specific subject areas – remember that you rarely have the opportunity to obtain the views of your clients en masse.

Some additional questions

Has there been any time when you have not been satisfied with the service you received from us?

If you can think of one thing that would most improve our service, what would that be?

CHAPTER SUMMARY

1.   Managers should establish the most important aspects of service for each of their client markets.

2.   Managers should regularly monitor and measure their clients' views on service levels on each of the important aspects of service.

3.   Managers must recognise the importance of obtaining clients' views and overcome resistance from fellow partners.

4.   Firms will require a management framework to support a client relationship programme.

5.   Firms should consider whether they have the expertise or time to conduct and analyse a survey to maximise the potential value from it.

6.   Firms should consider whether it would be cost-effective to obtain external assistance.

From research to actual improvement

- Consider how you are going to collate and analyse your data
- Have a central mechanism to collect information from key client interviews and review it across clients
- Choose a method of analysis and presentation to emphasise what clients are telling you
- Consult with those who will be affected by a change before implementing it
- Use action plans and allocate responsibilities and time limits for changes
- Use great tact when dealing with behavioural issues
- Be positive

Collating, analysing and presenting the results

The way in which you collate, analyse and present the results of data will depend on the method of collection you use.

Postal surveys

Although the volume of the data will be much greater with a questionnaire survey, it will be available altogether and should be analysed promptly. Closed, rating-scale questions can be analysed on a spreadsheet. You must present the results in such a way that perceived shortfalls in service delivery are apparent. Consider questions that represent an element of service together, those relating to managing billing or views on fee earners' commercial acumen for commercial clients for example, and then individually to ascertain where the greatest improvements are required. For instance, the following six questions represent managing billing (see Chapter 6).

1. *We discuss the basis of our charging with you at the beginning of the matter?*

2. *We agree with you at the outset how and when the matter is to be billed?*
3. *We discuss costs with you regularly throughout the matter?*
4. *Our bills are always in accordance with our agreement?*
5. *Our bills are presented in such a way that you can understand how they are calculated?*
6. *We are flexible in our approach to billing (commercial clients)?*

Analysing the firm's performance using the frequency of response to each score, and showing both the percentage of respondents who hold each view and the cumulative percentage, serves to emphasise the extent of any perceived shortfall of service. Table 8.1 highlights the impact this has when interpreting results.

Table 8.1   Frequency of results

We discuss the basis of charging at the outset

	Unsatisfactory	Needs improvement	Good	Very good	Excellent	Totals
	1	**2**	**3**	**4**	**5**	
No. of responses	20	20	36	12	4	92
Percentage of responses	22	22	39	13	4	100
Cumulative percentage	22	44	83	96	100	

Using percentages strengthens the evidence. Note that when the order of the questionnaire scoring is reversed to show 'unsatisfactory' on the left, it becomes apparent that 44 per cent of the clients surveyed were dissatisfied with the way this firm handled discussing the basis of charging at the outset of a matter. Had the scale also had greater variation around the mid-point (see Chapter 7, p. 71), it would be possible to gain greater insight into the thoughts of the 39 per cent of respondents who thought the firm were 'good' on this aspect of service.

Responses to the question asking commercial clients whether the firm's service is perceived as cost-effective are particularly important since many clients now instruct on a 'horses for courses' basis and are likely to leave a firm if they do not feel they are getting good value for money.

It is useful to understand the importance of the items of service represented by each question so that particular emphasis can be placed on getting the most important items right. If you also included a scale to measure the importance of the item, calculate the mean (average) value and show it alongside the frequency of perceptions.

Responses to open questions may be harder to analyse, but they often throw light on the responses to the closed questions and suggest ways in which improvements can be made. Collect them together on to one document and then check whether there are any glaring problems or any common themes in these responses. Responses to both open and closed questions should be interpreted together and conclusions drawn. They may show that your clients think you are wonderful. However, it is more likely that they will be a mixed bag with some good results, others not so good and some variation within responses if there are perceived inconsistencies in service delivery across fee earners. You have to identify perceived shortfalls in service and whether they are department specific or endemic throughout the firm.

Client interviews

It is less straightforward collating data from client interviews, particularly if more than one person undertakes them. Firms need a central mechanism by which such data can be collated, whether within the relevant team or department, or by the managing partner. If notes are not taken during the interviews, they should be made immediately afterwards. They should be full and cover the entire interview. The key points should be highlighted and decisions made on the appropriate way of rectifying any problem area. Specific agreements with the client on different or new ways of service delivery should be implemented immediately. You should look across data from the interviews of several clients to see if there are any common trends.

Focus groups

If focus groups of clients are used, the moderator will transcribe the results and, if sufficiently familiar with legal practice and your objectives, they should also be able to analyse the results to highlight what clients consider the firm is good at and what it needs to improve upon.

Whichever method of data collection you have used, you must interpret the results to decide where improvements need to be made and on the action to be taken to implement them.

What do you need to improve and how are you going to do it?

Having analysed the results, you must build up a picture of what changes are required to rectify any perceived shortfalls in your service. This step is probably the most difficult and you must give careful thought to the action you will take. What do the results tell you? Do you actually need to change what you do or is it a question of managing client expectations at the outset of a matter so that they are aware of what you can do for them? If change is required, is it a change of working processes and procedures or of behaviours, or both? What will you need to do to effect and sustain the change? What information do you need to give clients to manage their expectations and what additional training will fee earners need?

Having identified the problems you must consider *all* the issues that must be covered to effect the requisite changes. What are the implications of proposed changes? You need to consider not only the task itself but also organisational structures and lines of communication to support the change, new technology and finally, but by no means least, the likely effect on your people and how they will perceive the changes. What do you need to do in respect of each to bring about and sustain the desired change? Do not just tackle the easy procedural issues: behaviours will not change unless attitudes also change. For example, remedying fee earners' speed of response might involve:

- training for the fee earners to emphasise the importance of demonstrating speed of response;
- looking at the level of supervision they receive;
- considering the example set to them by the relevant partners or department heads;
- training for supervisors;
- looking at the firm's systems and procedures and ways of remedying the problem, including new ways of working;
- considering new technology to speed up getting work out;
- training for all involved in operating any new systems.

Prepare action plans in respect of each change to be effected and an overall review plan to ensure that all issues are dealt with. Allocate responsibilities and timescales for each plan. Ensure not only that the time of a review meeting is actually in everyone's diary, but that those involved also appreciate the importance of carrying out allocated tasks and of attending that meeting.

Changing behaviours will be harder because, depending upon the extent of the requisite change, sustaining it may require the same approach as that described in Chapters 10 and 11 on culture and motivation respectively in which these issues and overcoming resistance to change are discussed. You need to ensure that everyone is motivated to accept change and this will involve imparting an understanding of the reason for the change, and training. All aspects of management that have an impact will also have to be aligned to make sure there is no reversion to former ways: supervision, and appropriate competencies appraised for example. Identify skills gaps and training needs. What additional management skills are needed for example?

Presentation of results and feedback

Internally

Feedback to members of your firm must be from a positive stance. Blame and recrimination will not serve to change attitudes, but will only make people defensive and withdrawn. Your clients will doubtless think that you are excellent on some aspects of your service – give your people the praise they deserve for that and encourage them to bring all the aspects up to that level. But telling people to work harder or to improve will not bring about change – they need to be shown how to get there, to be led by the good example of partners and encouraged every step of the way.

Clients' views are a very forceful tool in making people realise the need for change. You must use whichever method of presentation will best drive home any message your clients are sending to you. Use percentages to emphasise the frequency of response as discussed earlier and present the information in graphic format if that assists. For example, if there is inconsistency in responses across departments, highlight them by using a bar chart, such as that used in Figure 8.1. However, bear your audience in mind because some solicitors are not pictorially minded and would rather have the results presented in words.

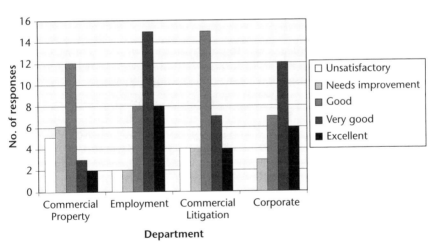

Figure 8.1   Perceptions of cost-effectiveness by department

Let your partners, fee earners and support staff know the procedural steps you propose to take to improve matters, and ask for feedback on any that involve them – are they practical: what else needs to be done to ensure they will work smoothly? Agree any changes in processes and procedures with the people who will operate them. Their understanding, cooperation and a common sense approach are essential for success.

Changing attitudes and consequent behaviours is far more difficult. Clients may tell you that they do not have confidence in some of your fee earners whose behaviour needs to be changed. Merely telling a person their attitude or behaviour is not what is desired does not assist. Such interviews need delicate and tactful handling because any adverse comment about the way in which a lawyer has dealt with any aspect of his or her professional work, including relationships with clients, will be upsetting to them. The individual needs to know not only exactly what the problem is, and why it is important to change, but also how their behaviour could change. Their strengths must be highlighted and the meeting always conducted in a positive manner.

To clients

Clients who participate in firms' surveys usually also want to know the results and the outcome. Do not be afraid to let them know – as long as you actually put any remedial steps into operation. Prepare a very short report of the key points and some of the actions you are implementing to bring about the requisite improvements – and remember to thank them for their involvement.

Sustaining changes

Sustaining change comes down to determination on the part of the leadership of the firm to make certain that your client service programme has the right profile of importance in the firm, and that things actually happen. Procedural changes can become effective in the short term; attitudinal changes are longer term and need constant support from the culture of the firm. Chapters 10 and 11 give a full discussion on achieving a client-oriented culture and motivating your people to accept change. The most successful firms will be those that are so aware of the important issues to clients that they will begin to think as a client and to understand fully their values. This process cannot be static: client markets change and individual commercial clients develop; firms need to develop with them. Training plays a vital role in client service because fee earners need to be regularly reminded of what is important to clients. Partners have to demonstrate by example and give guidance to ensure that the attitudes and behaviours of all fee earners will promote the development of client relationships. The requisite processes and procedures have to exist behind the scenes so that fee earners are able to give the desired level of service.

CHAPTER SUMMARY

1. Consider what you are trying to achieve, before you begin your research, and ensure that you have the commitment to carry out changes to your service delivery.
2. Consider how you are going to collate and analyse responses, before you conduct your research.
3. Do you have commitment from the partners to effect any requisite changes?
4. Present the results with the maximum impact to emphasise the need for change.
5. Ensure that all the implications of changes are considered so that they are sustainable.
6. Do not shirk from handling behavioural issues.
7. Be positive.

9

Which client markets?

KEY POINTS

- The importance of managerial capability to success
- Where should you be going? Your strategy and its implementation
- Planning must include the design of your service to match the needs of your target market and the resources of the firm, profitably
- Using a value curve to assess the price sensitivity of work

Profitability and managerial capability

The profession has increased by almost 50 per cent over the last three decades and there are now over 90,000 solicitors. The gap between high-street and 'magic circle' City firms has become so vast that they are almost different professions, but Table 9.1 shows that the gulf between successful firms, of all sizes, and the rest is also widening.

Table 9.1 Profits per equity partner, 1998–9. (Source: Law Society Panel Survey)

Size of firm	sole practitioners 1	2–4 partners 2	5–10 partners 3	11–25 partners 4	26–80 partners 5
Profit per equity partner			£000s		
Lower quartile	26	33	49	72	96
Median	46	56	62	98	167
Upper quartile	64	93	89	140	260

Although the general trend is that the larger the firm, the more profitable, the top 25 per cent of 2–4 partner firms have profits per equity partner in excess of £93,000, a higher upper-quartile figure than for 5–10 partner firms. However, in contrast, 25 per cent of 2–4 partner firms have profits of less than £33,000 per partner. Sole practitioners can also be successful – 25 per cent of them earn more than £64,000, whereas 25 per cent of firms with 11–25 partners have profits per partner of less than

£72,000. Why should this occur? Why are some firms successful and others not?

Some firms have a negative perspective of their future and such planning that is carried out usually involves continued introspection. Planning itself does not guarantee sustainable success; a failure to take account of providing value to clients will not maintain a level of profitability in the longer term. Firms need to have a focus, both on the client markets they are going to serve and on how they are going to serve them, profitably. For many firms, poor profits arise from either a lack of focus or a failure to design their service to meet the needs of the target client markets – ways of working in the past may no longer provide a desired level of profitability. The managerial capability of firms varies tremendously, as shown on the continuum in Figure 9.1.

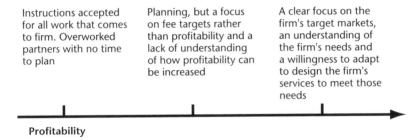

Figure 9.1   Managerial capability

Firms need management skills to:

- understand the overall concept of managing the practice to deliver a service that consistently meets clients' needs;
- interpret information, both internal and external to understand trends in client markets;
- interpret financial management information;
- plan, organise and control;
- manage people;
- communicate the firm's objectives to everyone in the firm;
- agree objectives for each individual to enable the firm to meet its objectives.

They also require organisational skills to ensure that:

- the firm's structure is designed to offer a service that will match the needs of the chosen client markets;
- the appropriate levels of supervision are in place;
- financial management reports contain only relevant information in a clear, simple format;

- lines of communication are established so that everyone in the firm understands the firm's objectives at any time;
- there is a mechanism for those in management to receive feedback from all within the firm;
- lines of communication are established to receive feedback on the firm's service from clients.

Your strategy

A firm needs to understand where it is at present before it can move forward to serve selected client markets effectively. This involves an analysis of both the internal elements of your firm (its resources and in particular your people and their skills) and the elements in the external market in which you operate. You need to understand the major limiting factors that will hinder the achievement of your objectives. All firms need to set objectives and goals, regardless of size and structure. Each department in a larger firm will have its own objectives, while still ensuring that the firm has a cohesive overall strategy. Objectives for smaller firms may in theory be easier to set, but, in reality, practitioners in those firms find it harder to find the time to plan. Nevertheless, it is essential that all firms take an objective look at their present position on a regular basis so that they are able not only to plan, but also to handle changes in the working environment and client markets, proactively rather than reactively. Do not get hung up on measuring success by financial management alone. A successful practice is based on a raft of factors and although sound financial management is essential, it is only one of them. The steps to be taken when making strategic decisions are outlined in Figure 9.2.

Not everything will go according to your plan and you need to keep checking on how you are doing vis-à-vis the bigger picture to ensure that you are still on the right track. Plans should not be regarded as written on tablets of stone, but seen as flexible. Events will happen that may throw you off course and may stop you achieving your aims in which case you can decide on your next course, but from a knowledgeable position. You should ask yourself what you are trying to achieve with regard to all your actions. Then ask yourself 'so what?', so that you consider the implications of what you are doing. Planning is an ongoing, four-stage process, as shown in Figure 9.3.

Some questions to address when considering your strategy

- Do all the partners share common values?
- What are your collective goals and aspirations?

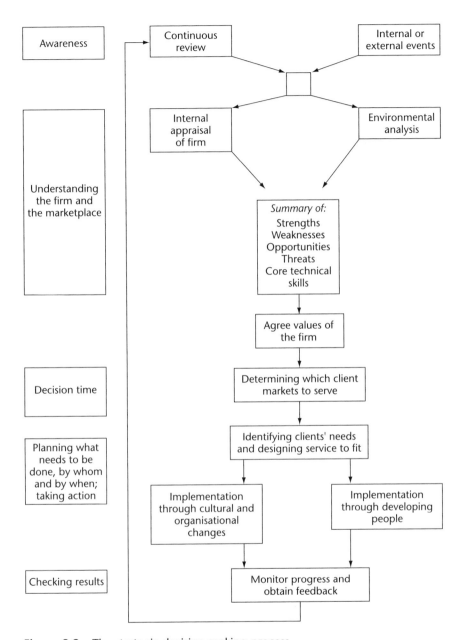

Figure 9.2   The strategic decision-making process

- What would be an attractive goal in say, three years' time, in terms of the number of partners and fee earners, client markets you are operating in and the gross fees and net profits?
- What services do you provide now?

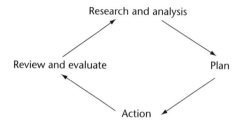

Figure 9.3   Four-stage planning process

- What services should you provide to meet your goals and objectives?
- How can you design delivery of your services to meet those objectives?
- How do you, as partners, perceive your practice, its competitive advantages and disadvantages?
- Are your perceptions realistic and objective?
- How does your perception fit with the perceptions of your clients and how will you find out what those are?
- Who are your fee earners and what are their specific talents?
- Which existing and potential client markets do you serve and what are their legal needs now and in the foreseeable future?
- Does the range of experience you have to offer meet the needs of your selected client markets?
- What are your strengths and weaknesses?

Present and future markets

- Which client markets do you compete in?
- What percentages of work come from repeat business and from referrals or recommendations?
- What are the market trends affecting the markets you serve and potentially could serve?
- What known external factors could impact on the market?
- What are the opportunities and growth potential of the markets as a whole?
- Who are your competitors and where are they located?
- What are the demographics of:

    - the members of your firm?
    - your clients?
    - the legal community within which you operate and would consider to be your competitors?

- How strong do you consider yourself relative to your competitor firms?
- What are your strengths v. your competitors' that will help you to exploit the potential in the market?

- What do your clients think of your service?
- What is your image/brand in the marketplace?
- What are the prevailing charge-out rates for the work types you provide, especially if the work types are regarded as 'commodity' services and therefore price sensitive?

Your practice

- How effective is the current management of the firm?
- How effective is the current structure of the firm?
- How good are your support staff?
- What are your internal communications like?
- How good are your management accounting systems?
- How good is your partners' level of understanding of financial issues relating to your practice?
- Do you make efficient and effective use of IT for accounting purposes and to manage client matters?
- How good are your systems for monitoring and supervising work?
- How efficient are the firm's administrative systems?
- How good is the firm at motivating and getting the most out of its people – support staff, fee earners and its partners?
- How do you use your training to enhance this?
- Assess the firm's financial results for the last three years, not only in terms of fees, but also in terms of profitability from various work types. Look to see whether there are any trends. How do your figures compare with those of similar-sized or types of firm? Do profit levels meet the desired expectations of your partners?

Work types

- How profitable is each work type?
- Could it be made more profitable by using a different level/mix of fee earners?
- Could it be more profitable by using IT more effectively?
- Are you pricing your services appropriately for the client markets you serve?

Your SWOT analysis

Consider your responses to each of the above points, but remember:

- be objective;
- concentrate on the big picture;
- set ambitious but realistic, achievable objectives;

- your strategy is not cast in stone and it should be constantly reviewed in the light of the changing environment.

Figure 9.4   SWOT analysis

Plot your responses to the questions as a strength or a weakness and give them a grading, e.g. A, B, C. Carrying out this exercise makes you really think about the nature of your practice and gives you a greater understanding of your current position. From your analysis, your strengths should indicate various options to you and you must then evaluate each and begin to implement your chosen course.

Implementation

Planning alone will not produce the desired results – there has to be action as well. Solicitors tend to be good at analysing and thinking about results, but not so good at acting on them. Management tasks facing a firm sometimes appear daunting, but if they are broken down into small, incremental stages, they are far more approachable. Having a simple action plan such as that in Figure 9.5 that allocates the task, responsibility and timescale is vital. Including the objective of the exercise helps to focus the mind, but keep it simple.

Activity	Responsibility	To be completed by	Relevant objective

Figure 9.5   Action plan

Designing your service to give value to clients

Part of your planning process should include how you are going to deliver each of your services to your chosen client markets. Your aim should be to design each service both to give perceived value to clients and to make a desired level of profit for the firm. By giving value to clients you will provide both short- and long-term value to the firm. Figure 9.6 demonstrates that it is a two-way process. Clients expect to receive value from legal services and the way in which they assess whether they have received value from you, including value for money, was discussed in Chapter 3. From the firm's point of view, value can be measured in hard terms: the number of recommendations and referrals, the value of work from a particular client or client market.

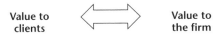

Value to clients   **Value to the firm**

Figure 9.6   Value to clients: a two-way process

In the short term, value for the firm is reflected in an increase in profitability arising from the ability to charge a proper fee because the work has been efficiently managed and effectively undertaken and fees have not been lost as a result of giving allowances to clients because of the poor management of files; in the longer term, it should manifest itself in:

- an increase in the client base;
- an enhanced reputation, image or brand;
- the potential to improve the quality of work;
- the ability to increase fees;
- the ability to attract and retain quality staff.

In the first place, however, you must deliver profitable services that clients both value and perceive as cost-effective. David McIntosh[1] broke down legal services into the following constituent parts:

- expert interpretation and application of legal knowledge;
- management of transactions or cases;
- personal client service.

The importance to the client of the mix of these parts depends on clients' perceptions of the importance of the matter or case to them and on their perceived level of risk. Thus legal services can be broadly categorised as follows:

1. Those that are extremely important to the client and carry a high level of perceived risk for which the client is prepared to pay the asking price.

2. Those that are of importance to the client and for which the client will pay a fair, negotiated price. Solicitors have to compete on service levels because numerous competitors offer similar expertise.

3. Those services that clients consider of a routine nature. Many are seen as 'commodities' including, for example, debt collection, remortgaging or other matters where the work is not of perceived high risk. These matters are highly price sensitive and clients are frequently only prepared to pay a fixed price.

Regardless of category and price, clients will still want a prompt and reliable service and it is becoming increasingly hard to maintain levels of both service and profits. Successful firms still do so by focusing on the client market they are serving and designing their services with the appropriate level and mix of fee earners backed up by the effective use of IT to ensure profitability.

Unfortunately, there is only a small amount of work available in the first category, and few solicitors with the requisite level of expertise. The increase in numbers in the profession has resulted in too many practices providing the same range of services of work in the second category and the only way for firms to differentiate themselves is on the service given to clients. Work in the third category can be profitable, but not through traditional working practices.

The value curve in Figure 9.7 shows the value of legal services relative to the amount of work available. The greater the volume of work, the more solicitors there are with the ability to undertake that work, which in turn leads to market forces pushing down the price.

Use the graph to gain a greater understanding of the particular work types your firm undertakes and potential pricing structures. Although sections on the curve other than 'commodities' may have greater relevance to larger firms acting for commercial clients, all firms can use the curve to make an objective assessment of their work types by plotting them on the graph and considering how they should deliver their service. Each work type is likely to have its own value curve, depending on the level of price sensitivity. However, bear in mind that offering low prices may be appropriate if you are a new entrant into a market, but, depending on your location, your work may be less price sensitive than you think if most of it comes from repeat business or recommendation.

Different segments of the same market may lie at different places on the curve. The way in which your departments or teams are structured should reflect the needs of whichever segment you have chosen to serve. For example, low-price conveyancing will be at the far right hand of the 'commodities' section, whereas the segment of the domestic conveyanc-

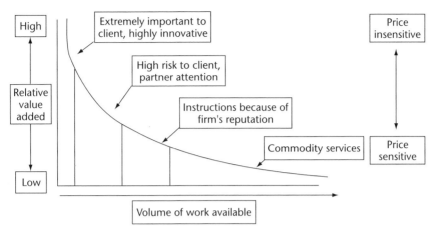

Figure 9.7   The value curve
Source: Adapted from William C. Cobb's Value Curve adapted in R. C. Reed (1992) *Win-Win Billing Strategies: Alternatives That Satisfy Your Clients and You,* American Bar Association. Reproduced by permission.

ing market that is prepared to pay for a greater contact level of service can be plotted nearer the left-hand edge of that section. Delivering low-price conveyancing requires using lower levels of fee earner, an effective use of IT and comparatively cheap accommodation. It is essential to have the right level of salary cost if the work is to be profitable, but junior fee earners can deliver an excellent level of service to clients, with the requisite training, supervision and motivation. It takes courage for smaller firms to take on additional fee earners at the right level, but careful analysis before plans are made will remove much of the element of risk.

However, if you are a general high-street practice and most of your conveyancing work comes from existing clients, it will probably be less price sensitive. Have the courage to increase your fees and consider reducing costs to the firm by working in teams. In some firms, for instance, a partner or senior fee earner handles matters up to and including exchange of contracts and then the file is handed over to a paralegal who deals with the completion and post-completion stages. Most clients are happy with this arrangement providing that it is sold to them at the outset, they meet the other member of the team and they understand that, should any problem occur, the file will be passed back to the experienced fee earner. A lot of good former conveyancing secretaries who might otherwise be redundant with the increased use of IT have retrained as paralegals. You may not win every quote by increasing your rates, but do you really want to? Is it not better to have slightly fewer clients and to be able to process their matters effectively, efficiently and profitably?

Remember that the profitability of fee income and not the fee income alone is the important measure. How much is it costing you to produce the work? Firms need to rethink their working practices. Working long hours and being extremely busy does not equate either to being profitable or to giving a good service to clients. What counts is working efficiently and effectively so that clients can be given the level of service they seek. Depending on the profitability of each work type, ask yourself the following questions:

- Are you expanding the right types of work in the first place?
- Are you using the right level of fee earner?
- What is the level of fee earner required?
- Can you possibly be profitable using that mix of partners and fee earners?
- Are you making the most effective use of your existing IT?
- Would an investment in IT allow you to become profitable?
- Would that allow you to provide a service that your clients want?
- How well do you manage knowledge and information in the firm?
- Do your fee earners need greater training?
- Do your fee earners have too many files to undertake the work proactively, or are they constantly fire-fighting, working inefficiently and giving a poor service to clients?
- Do you have adequate file review systems in place?

Managing fee earners

Although there are aspects of practice management for which it is possible to specify procedures, the solicitor–client relationship is people based and it is impossible to lay down hard and fast rules relating to how to conduct human relationships. It is particularly difficult to manage a group of solicitors whose professionalism, training, the nature of their work and the ownership of their client base, makes them autonomous individuals. To ensure a consistent service, it is vital that everyone in the firm is aware of the aspects of service that create client confidence. Managers should ensure that fee earners in particular:

- receive the appropriate level of supervision;
- do not have too many files to be able to work effectively;
- are given regular training on client service to remind them of a client's perspective and the importance of getting the delivery right for the benefit of both client and firm.

Knowledge management

Firms of all sizes are recognising the benefits of implementing a knowledge management system that allows fee earners easy access to all the knowledge and information they need to deliver an efficient and effective service to clients. Such systems involve the integration of different systems and applications relating to document and case management, practice management, the accounts function, Internet access, e-mail, portals and external information. In a survey of firms[2] that had implemented knowledge management initiatives, the firms measured success in terms of client satisfaction, increased profits and an improved competitive position and viewed knowledge management as part of their overall business strategy that has to be integrated into the culture of the firm. Management support and firm-wide acceptance are crucial to the success of such initiatives.

CHAPTER SUMMARY

1. Firms must appreciate the importance of managerial capability to success.

2. A firm must focus on specific services for specific client markets following a thorough analysis of its current internal and external position and anticipated factors.

3. Each service must be designed to fit the needs of both the target market and the firm.

4. Planning must take account of the perceived value and price sensitivity of each service to clients.

5. Firms must recognise the importance of supervision and training.

Notes

1   D. McIntosh, 'Professional pride', see [2001] *Gazette*, 1 November, 21.
2   'Managing partner and perceptive technology, KM survey 2002', *Managing Partner*, September 2002, 5(4), p.14.

10

Achieving a client-oriented culture

KEY POINTS

- Culture plays a significant role in a firm's ability to consistently deliver excellent service
- Culture defined
- Culture is set by the partners of a firm
- Partners must have a genuine commitment to client service and lead by example
- Managing people is crucial to their acceptance of change
- Strong leadership and careful planning are vital when trying to effect a change of culture

Culture: creating a climate for performance

It is attitudes that drive financial results and not the other way round.[1]

To survive and compete in today's marketplace, a firm must be able to respond quickly to external change and to be able to think imaginatively about its services and the way in which it offers them to consistently meet clients' needs and to maintain profitability. Firms must recognise that providing legal services in line with those needs forms the core of their business: technical competence is no longer enough. Considering the client first must be second nature to everyone in the firm. Those firms that remain complacent and continue to be inward looking will be overtaken by events and will lose clients. Innovation and a willingness to change are prerequisites for sustainable growth and firms must be receptive to both.

It is hard to sustain the delivery of excellent client service without an effective culture: one that is based on openness and trust, honest communication and feedback, and teamwork, and where relationships between members are good and internal politics and struggles for power are absent. For instance, teamworking will struggle to survive in an atmosphere of aggressive individual target-based competition in which fee earners are reluctant to delegate files. Every member of a firm should understand and feel secure in their role in the firm. Friendly, informal practices work if they are backed by adequate supervision and support. They fail if people are left to struggle on their own because partners are too busy to delegate well, to listen to the concerns of their staff or to appreciate what their staff are capable of.

Although Mark Hastings,[2] Policy Advisor of the Institute of Management was speaking of business-to-business services, his comments are equally relevant to steps to effect the development of relationships with both business and private clients of legal practices:

> Clients want to see a much greater involvement and commitment from their service providers in finding solutions to their business needs. Fees now reflect results, so suppliers have every incentive to manage those relationships well. Even when relationship managers are appointed, it often doesn't work because the person doesn't get the right back up. It requires a transformation of attitude to become a relationship-management culture.

Andrew Brown[3] describes culture as something that an organisation 'is' rather than something that an organisation 'has'. For a legal firm it is the shared beliefs, attitudes and values that exist within it and, because the primary influences on its culture are the characters, personalities and skills of its partners and people, no two firms are alike. It sets the scene for the way in which the firm delivers its services to its clients, and the consistency of that service. The features of service that create confidence and value for clients relate back to a firm's culture: its ethos, organisational structures, levels of supervision, continuity of staff and all the issues that lie behind a client focus are influenced by the values of the firm, by 'the way we do things round here'. To give clients the added value they seek, firms must put clients at the heart of everything that the firm does. All its members should understand clients' needs and giving a service that meets them should be second nature. It is up to the partners to create the climate for this to be achieved. This may involve a rethink not only of the way in which a practice is managed and structured but also of prevailing attitudes and behaviours.

Financial performance targets have become the conventional primary strategy for improving profitability in the profession but neglecting culture for the sake of driving up profits may be a very short-term approach. It may also be at a high cost to the firm itself: increased productivity does not necessarily lead to increased profitability. The cost of demotivated staff and consequent high staff turnover, poor client service and the potential risk of negligence claims must also be taken into account. How long can a culture that is solely profit driven be sustained in terms of people who are overworked and stressed and no longer enjoy work? Firms cannot rely on financial management alone because all information is sensitive to the context within which it exists. It is a question of getting the balance right, between the harder issues that are quantitative and measurable, and the softer issues relating to people and clients. Successful firms do have sound financial management and the ability to interpret it but they also set and maintain high standards and have a culture that inspires and enables their people to give an excellent service.

Culture lies at the root of what a partnership is about. The leaders of any organisation are largely responsible for its culture; without leadership, there is no one to set a standard for others to follow. It is up to the partners of a legal firm collectively, as owners of their business, to decide on what they want the core values of their partnership to be. This does not mean the issue of a bland and meaningless mission statement, but requires a meaningful discussion of the type of practice they want and an agreement as to the shared values that they want their practice to have. Having such a discussion may not be easy and may involve addressing issues that have previously not been confronted, including levels of commitment from partners themselves. But it is worth it – taking this step will give a partnership a clearer vision of what the firm stands for and where it wants to be, rather than being bogged down in day-to-day activities. It is not a complicated process although it may create difficulties in some partnerships. Nevertheless, it should not be avoided. Where does the emphasis lie? Are there any desired values that are discordant with the majority? It is hoped that you will have consistency, but do not be afraid to have a full and open discussion on *all* views. Sweeping them under the carpet, again, will not promote long-term trust and openness.

Although many practices will share common values, the emphasis will vary in each. Delivering an excellent service to clients within the firm's target markets must be a prerequisite for any firm. Similarly, values of openness and trust and the development of the firm's people through consultation, participation and education are essential for success. Future decisions can be made against the agreed set of values and, although each department and office will develop its own subculture, all will share the common core values. It is up to all the partners to communicate actively those values, both internally and externally, directly and indirectly, and to lead by example. For instance, those values should form the basis of the competencies in appraisal or bonus systems. Without a clear statement of the values the partners stand for, other members of a firm will not know what to do and how to do it or what to say to clients and how to say it.

Agreeing a set of values alone will not make you successful. A change of culture is an ongoing process that needs constant reinforcement by the behaviour and commitment of partners to sustain it. Partners are effectively role models from whom other members of a firm take their cue for their own attitudes and behaviours and to expect consistency in delivering excellent service from everyone in a firm, the partners themselves have to set the standards and be consistent in their own behaviour.

Paying lip-service to client service will not be enough. Partners' behaviour and commitment must be genuine and authentic to motivate and influence others. Without leadership, there is no one to set a standard for others to follow.

However, the first task in the process of change to a client-oriented culture may be to unfreeze the attitudes of partners so that they not only become receptive to innovation and change but that they are actually committed to it. They must be dissuaded from considering these issues as the latest management buzzwords and convinced of the merits of viewing them as part of their ongoing thinking about the way in which they work. This may not be easy. Solicitors are autonomous professionals who, by and large, enjoy their technical work but whose training and the nature of that work naturally result in them being cautious and risk averse. An entrepreneurial solicitor is a rare thing. Few have had any formal management training and many view management solely as administration without grasping that it involves seeing the bigger picture of the firm within the context of its external environment, deciding appropriate objectives and guiding it on a route to achieve them. Many solicitors are overworked and uninterested in management per se. Some, however, are far sighted and prove excellent managers if allowed by their fellow partners. Unfortunately, the flat management structure of most firms can lead to resistance to progress and change. David Maister takes a stronger line.[4] He considers that the real problem facing legal partnerships is that 75 per cent of partners are 'cruisers', good solid citizens who pretend to be interested in supervision and to a commitment to client service, but in reality they have no real appetite for success. They come in, work hard professionally and make an adequate living. They concentrate on financial management, but they are not interested in strategic management or where the firm is going in the future.

> The way you make money in business is not to be good at managing the money. The way you get money in business is to decide what you want to compete on . . . and once you've decided what it is you want to be, the key to making the money is enforcing the standards appropriate for that choice.[5]

To be successful, firms have to agree appropriate rights and responsibilities for their partners and those partners must be prepared to be accountable to the partnership for their delivery. Pretence that they are interested in supervision, communication or appraisals and that they have a commitment to client service is not enough. Writing a mission statement setting out the firm's objectives will not achieve those objectives. There has to be genuine commitment and accountability.

Leadership

It is difficult to effect change, particularly in the attitudes of partners, without strong leadership. Recent research has shown that two-thirds of management initiatives do not produce the hoped-for results. Businesses do not have a good track record for sustaining change or of overcoming the frequent cynicism with which it is met. To succeed, there has to be a greater understanding not only of the limiting factors that hinder change, but also of the processes that reinforce its growth and what acts as a catalyst for it. In legal practices, the greatest restricting factor will be resistance to change from its people. Therefore how people are managed will be crucial to success. A benevolent dictator who ignores poor performance and sweeps difficult issues under the carpet will not earn the respect of fellow partners or staff and will gradually serve to demotivate members of the firm. Similarly, a senior or managing partner who corrects or betters people's efforts, or who takes the recognition for those efforts, will stifle initiative. Why should people bother? Every leader brings different qualities to the post, but the following are some that they will need to effect change in attitudes and behaviours.

People generally want to feel part of a successful team that knows where it is heading. Therefore leaders must consistently pursue the clear vision of what they want to achieve, and must be able to convey that vision and share their enthusiasm and drive with others. Most people rise to a challenge, as long as they understand the potential benefits and the real obstacles that may have to be overcome to achieve them. One person alone cannot bring about a change in the attitudes and behaviours of everyone else and a leader will need the support of people at all levels in the firm.

A leader trying to effect change will have to be fairly tough skinned and not take differences of opinion as personal criticism. Good debate is healthy. Above all, a successful leader will be able to communicate: not only to impart his or her ideas but to listen to the concerns of others and to reassure. Resistance will often arise because of fear of the unknown. It is up to a leader to dispel those fears by listening to and understanding them. If a leader does not communicate, then that lender will not understand how to motivate others, including other partners with whom he or she must always remain in touch to be able to understand their current thinking and concerns. John Harvey-Jones[6] suggests that durable leadership is based on two-way communication: projecting your own views but also being able to hear the views that come back to you.

Leaders need to be totally committed and determined to succeed and prepared to confront those that do not want to buy into new ways, but they must still listen to everyone else's views and be open to new ideas from all sources, including the most junior member of staff. Michael Shaw of Cobbetts[7] considers respect to be a key issue in leadership, not for the leader, but by the leader for *everyone* in the firm. Not all new ideas will work and what works in one firm will not necessarily work in another, but leaders must have the courage, and support, to innovate and, if necessary, to learn from mistakes. If partners are seen to discuss their own problem files, it will encourage other fee earners to do likewise. If people are to give of their best, they must not feel threatened. Treating their mistakes as failures will result in non-disclosure of problems whereas treating them as a learning process will promote greater openness. That is not to say that partners should not discipline those whose work is substandard either from laziness or ineptitude because that will affect client service.

Leaders have to accept that they individually are not the reason for the success of the firm because, above all, they should put the interests of the people within the firm before their own. Sven-Goran Eriksson is not a loud, charismatic character but someone who is prepared to allow the members of the England team to develop to their full potential. Similarly, the successful leader of a legal practice has to allow the natural talents of its members to develop and grow to allow the firm to evolve constantly to keep pace with clients' changing needs. It is essential to nurture staff, to recognise the potential of even the most junior of them, and to bring out the best in all of them.

In legal services, knowledge creates power. Leaders actively encourage openness by sharing their own knowledge and encouraging others to do likewise. Knowledge is also a firm's greatest asset. By sharing knowledge, a firm can improve the depth of expertise offered to clients and enhance its reputation.

Leading a firm for the future involves more than just managing it for the present. Some significant differences between leaders and managers[8] are set out in Table 10.1.

Although a marketing department is likely to play a significant part in the practical aspects of a client service programme, driving through the process of a change in attitudes and behaviours should not be assigned to a marketing manager, or a practice manager, however able and well qualified the person. He or she is likely to be unable to overcome resistance from professionals who claim to know how to look after their clients better than any non-professional. Nor should the marketing partner be the obvious choice as leader despite having shown an aptitude for developing client relationships – an interest in marketing does not necessarily mean they have the attributes of leader.

To ensure that a legal practice can deliver excellent service to its clients, effective leadership must:

1. Ensure that everyone in the firm has a clear vision of what they are aiming to accomplish and the impact that will have on the firm's organisation, its members and its clients.

Table 10.1   Managers and leaders

Managers and leaders: spot the difference	
Manager	**Leader**
Is a copy	Is an original
Administers	Innovates
Maintains	Develops
Focuses on systems and structure	Focuses on people
Relies on control	Inspires trust
Has short-range view	Has long-range perspective
Asks how and when	Asks what and why
Has his/her eye on the bottom line	Has his/her eye on the horizon
Accepts the status quo	Challenges the status quo
Is the classic good soldier	Is his/her own person
Does things right	Does the right thing

Source: First Crédit Suisse Bank, *Sunday Times,* 8 July 2001

2. Establish direction by communicating clear goals and objectives for everyone in the firm, linked to the firm's business plan and departmental plans.
3. Enable everyone in the firm to have clarity in terms of their role, their objectives, their performance and how or where they can add value in the provision of excellent client service, making clear what is expected and creating an environment in which client-focused behaviour and initiative is encouraged.
4. Ensure that everyone in the firm sees the value of their efforts is appropriately recognised and rewarded.
5. Make sure that all members of the firm have the support and guidance that are needed to perform effectively and to develop their capabilities.
6. Ensure that all members of the firm have the requisite skills and competencies, both technical and managerial, to enable the firm to deliver an excellent service to clients.

Managing the change

A culture cannot be changed overnight but it can be modified gradually, over time.

> Cultural change is a slow process, it can be assisted rather than controlled but, in given circumstances, its pursuit might be worth while as long as it is not sought as a facile, cosmetic and transitory change.[9]

The process of change will need to be managed and constantly re-enforced so that new ways do not slip and ingrained habits allowed to re-emerge. It is particularly difficult to manage and maintain momentum in a longstanding project when fee-earning work will inevitably take priority on occasions. Strong leadership from a person dedicated to achieving success is essential to ensure that matters are not allowed to slip because of the pressure of work. Nick Jarrett-Kerr,[10] former chief executive of Bevan Ashford, who successfully instituted a client care programme in that firm, emphasised the importance of his role in project-managing it throughout to ensure that it stayed on course. Even if a firm uses outside consultants to advise and help with the design of a client service pro-gramme, it is up to the partners and leaders within the firm to communicate *their* values, to lead by example and to manage the process of the change, on an ongoing basis. Change cannot be forced or driven through. It can only be brought about when you have motivated your staff sufficiently not only to accept your values but also to live by them.

Managing change requires research and planning using a logical and common sense approach. Actually starting will probably be the hardest thing, but firms should begin by establishing the issues that they need to change. They should ensure that they build in regular reviews of what has been achieved at each stage in the context of the overall project. Review the progress of each section frequently and your project overall slightly less often to ensure that it is still on track. Consider:

- What do we want to change?
- Why do we need to change it?
- How are we going to change it?
- How are we going to assess whether we have been successful?

Remember to consider the implications of all your actions – the 'so what' factor. Good management is not about predicting the future in exact terms but in understanding the likely implications of what will happen if certain actions are taken or are not taken on all other aspects of practice management. All are interrelated and need to be in alignment to achieve your goals. Otherwise, they will give mixed messages both internally or externally.

Break down what you want to do into small sections. Set objectives for each:

- What do you want to achieve?
- By when?
- Who is to be involved?
- Who is to be responsible?

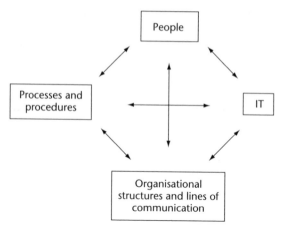

Figure 10.1   The interrelationships between a firm's resources

A step-by-step approach to changing culture

Each firm comprises a group of individuals with different personalities and professional skills, different clients, desires, needs and resources, and therefore the problems faced by each are unique. Thus each has to work out the best way of adopting an innovative, client-oriented culture that fits its people and circumstances. However, there are many common factors that influence whether the espoused values of partners are actually followed in day-to-day happenings in a firm – its organisational structures, leadership at varying levels, lines of communication, formal and informal reward systems and delegation and supervision, among others. The following model (Figure 10.2) is an outline guide for firms of all sizes to use when considering the issues that will impact on the sustainability of change. As such, it is a helpful starting point.

Stage 1: Understanding the existing culture

What are you trying to change, and why? In the model, the first stage is shown as the time during which the partners gain an understanding of the firm's existing culture. You cannot assume that you know what it is because unless shared values have been actively communicated throughout a firm in the past, your firm may have different cultures in each department, or team, and almost certainly in different offices, if you have more than one. Instead, begin to understand the existing culture by talking informally to staff and key personnel, and by observing. By looking at the nature of the politics and power plays between individuals and within groups, it is possible to establish who are the key influencers in a firm, at all levels and in each office, team or department. A questionnaire

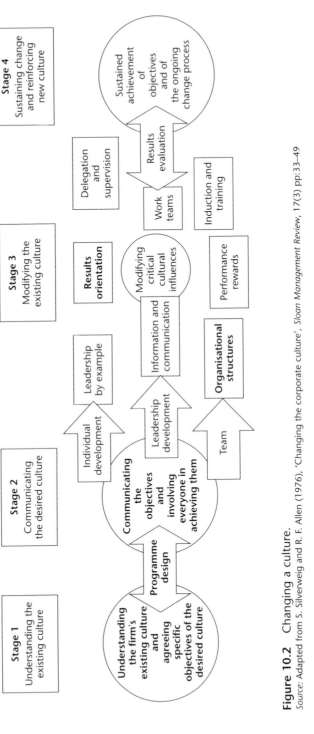

Figure 10.2 Changing a culture.

Source: Adapted from S. Silverweig and R. F. Allen (1976), 'Changing the corporate culture', *Sloan Management Review*, 17(3) pp:33–49 (see the example in the Annex, pp. 109–12) for completion by everyone in the firm can provide very useful insights. Anonymity of response will make people freer with comments, but it is useful to know the office, department and status of the respondent. However, remember that the consideration of the responses will only give an interpretation of the culture and that interpretation will be subjective. Everyone in the firm should complete the questionnaire to get as balanced a picture as possible.

Having gained an understanding of the current culture, partners should be able to establish the extent of any gap between this and any new core values that they want their firm to embody. There are also likely to be certain ingrained practices that the firm wishes to change. Note the principal points of difference, and consider ways of closing the gaps. What should your key objectives be? Keep them as simple as possible because everyone in the firm will have to understand what you are seeking to achieve. The gap may vary across offices or departments and the weightings attached to each may require different emphasis.

At the end of your enquiries, you should be able to answer the following points with some degree of certainty:

- What is the existing culture in the firm?
- Is it common throughout the firm?
- What are the gaps between where we are now and what we want to be?
- Are the proposed changes in line with the needs of the client markets we have chosen to serve in our business plan?
- What is our plan of action to close those gaps?

Stage 2: Communicating the desired culture

The second stage of the model relates to the communication of the new values to *everyone* in the firm, from senior partner to office junior. It is often easier to communicate and involve everyone in a smaller firm, but larger firms will generally be broken down into smaller teams or departmental units in any event. Bear in mind that although partners and heads of departments are sound lawyers, they are not trained human resource managers nor are they all natural communicators. They may need coaching and developing themselves to fulfil their role. Modifying a culture will only be brought about by an acceptance of the new values and consequent changes in the attitudes and behaviours of individuals, their leaders and within teams.

Stage 3: Modifying the existing culture

The whole firm will develop as individuals change and develop and therefore steps have to be taken to encourage actively their learning and development. Focusing on personal and professional development will benefit both the practice and the individual and will ultimately have the effect of modifying the culture. The areas that will have the greatest impact on bringing about and sustaining the changes are detailed in Stage 3 of the model.

1. Leaders in each team or department play a vital role in disseminating the message. They exercise power and influence through words and action and set an example by their own behaviour towards clients. If the firm's partners, management or team leaders appear uninterested and uncommunicative, staff will find it difficult to express their views and suggestions for improvements in working practices. Leaders of teams will need to take time to communicate with others in their team and to listen to their concerns so that an open, honest exchange can take place in which needs, aspirations, issues and ideas for change can be discussed.

   Information and communication systems: cultures are supported by the communication of the information that you want the rest of the firm to support. Most solicitors work individually and communication is often poor within a firm. If you do not tell staff what you want to achieve and explain their role in that achievement, there will be a breakdown in communication. Lines of communication and responsibilities need to be established at the outset and teams can form the backbone to them. These lines must allow for two-way communication. It takes courage to receive 360° feedback but, handled well and acted upon, it can strengthen a firm. It is not only fee earners that have ideas for improving the efficiency and effectiveness of the way in which work is processed.

2. Organisational structures, policies, budgets and procedures, formal and informal reward systems all convey important messages from the power structure in the firm to staff about the firm's cultural priorities – by the way it is managed and led by the partners. It is essential that a firm avoids disparity between its stated aims and what actually happens. For instance, what is considered in regular supervision meetings and *how* it is discussed sends messages to those being supervised. Beware, too, of a silo culture within a firm – see Figure 10.3. This can be prevalent in practices that emphasise competition between departments in relation to achieving targets for example. Members of a department often feel greater loyalty to their department than to the firm and there is little contact or cross-fertilisation of work or of ideas between departments. Lines of communication are vertical and new lines need to be set up at all levels *across* departments.

3. Performance and reward systems: what is appraised and rewarded influences the culture of the firm. When designing appraisals, give consideration to the weights assigned to attributes relating to the assessment of skills, behaviours, including client-related behaviours, and

Commercial   Probate   Family   Litigation

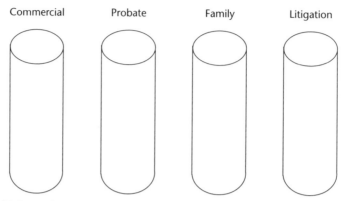

Figure 10.3 A departmental silo culture

results, to ensure that they mirror the values espoused by the partners and the desired culture of the firm. Firms with enlightened people-management policies are increasingly appraising staff against frameworks of competencies, appropriate to the particular level or grade, that relate to the development of the individual for the benefit of the firm. For example for fee earners competencies might relate (inter alia) to analysis and problem solving, innovation and judgemental skills, an awareness of clients' needs, communication skills, commercial awareness (if appropriate), teamworking, time management and self-motivation. For those in a leadership position, these could be extended to the ability to develop others, influence and persuade, supervision, business development and administration. Emphasis should be on the future: first, what individuals need to know next to be able to better fulfil their role within the firm and, second, what the firm needs to do to enhance the motivation of individuals to achieve that role.

Firms should consider the effect of the basis of their bonus systems. If only financial-target based, do they convey the message that that is the firm's prime objective? Are they based on individual performance, team-based performance or overall firm performance, or a combination? If you want members of a team to succeed as a team, you must reward them as a team, otherwise individual fee earners will hold on to work that should be passed across to another fee earner. Perceived fairness and consistency play a significant part in the motivational aspect of any reward system. The efforts of support staff enable fee earners to deliver a service to clients, and bonus systems that extend to all members of a team are perceived as fairer, and therefore more cohesive.

4. Induction and training provide opportunities to influence culture. Induction is an ideal time to inform a new recruit about the firm, what it stands for and what its values are, rather than concentrating

solely on the internal mechanics of the firm. Whenever a person joins from another firm, it is important to ensure that he or she becomes moulded into the way in which the firm works and does not import adverse influences into it. Induction should not merely be the first day, but should be ongoing over the first two or three months.

Giving excellent service to clients is a skill that has to be acquired by everyone in a firm – it cannot be delegated to another department. Training is the only way in which you can ensure that everyone understands the meaning of excellent service and what has to be done to deliver it. Therefore it must be seen as an investment and not a cost and your training budget should be as large as you can possibly afford. A survey of clients is likely to reveal aspects of your service that could be improved and people will need training either in relation to behaviours or in new ways of working. Because lawyers tend to concentrate on what they are saying and not how they are saying it, many need training in communication skills, including listening skills. The aim should be to give value to clients through communication. Partners and heads of departments may need staff development coaching or guidance, or interpersonal or supervisory skills. Training should be linked to appraisals which, if conducted well, will highlight other training needs for all levels of your staff. Appropriate training should be motivational and lead to a general improvement in morale in the firm. To lead to a better and more productive use of the practice's resources, training should be planned and training needs should be assessed not only at an individual level but in the light of the objectives of the department and of the firm.

5. Teamwork culture: working in teams plays a vital role in achieving the balance between delivering excellent service and maintaining the profitability of the firm. All teams have their own subculture, which may have to be specifically influenced and moulded to ensure that it makes a positive contribution to the new culture, even down to the working relationship between fee earner and secretary that usually develops ad hoc without external input. Regular meetings between partners or management and heads of teams are essential to ensure that the message to be conveyed is fully understood and is being disseminated. Teams should include everyone associated with the client or work type, including the most junior member. Managers in firms often say that their staff are not interested in anything beyond coming in, doing their work and getting paid for it. However, if you ask the staff directly, the message is usually quite different. Most people want to be involved in achieving something and, if they understand your aims, they will work with you to achieve them.

6. Delegation and supervision: downward delegation and supervision offer opportunities to influence culture through coaching and when setting the standards to which work must be performed. Effective

delegation involves objectives, terms of reference back and boundaries of responsibility, all of which can be set with a focus on delivering excellent service to clients. The Legal Services Commission Standards and requirements of Lexcel accreditation relating to supervision share the objective of providing an accurate and reliable service to clients.

7. Results orientation: having a set of criteria against which your initial objectives overall and for each area in which you are implementing changes can be measured, provides some sort of tangible evidence of progress you have achieved, will be motivational to 'the converted' but more importantly, will help to win over the sceptics. But, beware: although some pundits argue that what is not measurable does not get done, it is not possible to create meaningful measures for everything, particularly the softer behavioural issues. These results will be longer term and will be seen in improved ratings from clients and in increased loyalty and referrals.

Stage 4: Sustaining the desired culture

Leadership is essential for the constant reinforcement of a culture. Attitudes in the firm will not change overnight but the emphasis must be on developing people. Communication and training play a vital part in any programme of change. There has to be both an acceptance of the new values *and* a complementary change in behaviour. Not only do you have to gain recognition and agreement that new ways of working are better but you have to take steps to ensure that the new ways actually take the place of ingrained habits and that individuals have the skills and knowledge to put them into effect (see Figure 10.4). Peter Senge[11] advocates that the key catalyst for the development of a learning organisation is the development of the learning capabilities of its members. It is an ongoing and continuous process of improvement, the result of which will be that the firm will be open to new opportunities, and its members more willing to adapt to take on board new ideas and ways of working and not be fearful of change.

No one claims that changing attitudes is easy, particularly when people genuinely belive that those existing attitudes are right. Overcoming the fear of change combined with the natures of professionals themselves will probably be the greatest hurdle. Management training to acquire the requisite competencies can be obtained, but it all takes time, a luxury not available to many smaller firms. But these are all negative views, which will take us nowhere. What you need is a will to succeed – with that you can achieve anything.

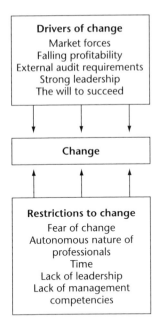

Figure 10.4 Sustaining change

The benefits of a change to a client-oriented culture

The benefits are threefold. For clients, these will be improved consistency and reliability of service and an awareness of and better responsiveness to their changing needs. For the firm, creating a positive culture that inspires and enables individuals to deliver an excellent service to target client markets whose needs are understood will have long-term beneficial effects on profitability, through client loyalty and the attraction of new work. For staff, it will give a better perception of adding value to the service they give to clients. The sense of being part of a team effort, greater motivation in a positive environment and a greater pride in their own work and in the firm will also act as a catalyst for improved staff morale and greater loyalty. Altogether, the firm will be a happier place in which to work. Dennis Healey made the remark 'When you are in a hole, stop digging'. Firms should get their culture right before spending vast sums on new computer systems, which will not change the attitudes of those using them.

CHAPTER SUMMARY

1.   Managers must recognise that, unless attitudes are changed, any driven change will be unsustainable.

2.   Partners need to agree the key values of their partnership and to use those values as the foundation for change.

3.   Leadership is vital, but leaders do not need to be dominant, forceful personalities. They do need to have determination and a will to win.

4.   Plan how to manage change, understand what you need to change and approach it in small chunks.

5.   To sustain change, all aspects of practice management must be in line to support the desired culture.

6.   Partners must lead by example.

Notes

1   D. Maister (2001) *Practice What You Preach: What Managers Must Do to Create a High Achievement Culture*, Free Press.
2   *Sunday Times*, 5 September 1999.
3   A. Brown (1998) *Organisational Culture*, Pearson Education Limited.
4   D. Maister, 'The problem of standards', *Managing Partner*, December 2001–January 2002 4(7), p.34.
5   Ibid.
6   J. Harvey-Jones, 'Great expectations', *Ambassador*, Association of MBAs, March 2001, p.10.
7   M. Shaw, 'Cereal packet leadership', *Managing Partner*, July/August 2001 4(3), p.6.
8   First Crédit Suisse Bank, *Sunday Times*, 8 July 2001. © Tmes Newspapers Limited.
9   P. Anthony (1994) *Managing Culture*, Open University Press.
10   N. Jarrett-Kerr, 'Showing that you care', *Managing for Success*, law management section, March 2000.
11   P. Senge, *et al.* (1999) *The Dance of Change: The Challenges of Sustaining Momentum in Learning Organisations*, Nicholas Brealey Publishing Ltd.

Annex: Questionnaire to assess current culture

No.	Orientation and culture	Definitely true	Mostly true	Mostly false	Definitely false
1	**Information and communication orientation**				
1a	The firm communicates effectively with staff				
1b	Individuals tend to keep information to themselves				
1c	Fee earners generally give full information when transferring files to other fee earners				
1d	Team leaders promote two-way dialogue with their team members				
1e	Important information usually finds its way to those who need to know it				
1f	Disruptive gossip and speculation are rife here				
2	**Creativity and innovation orientation**				
2a	People here are generally imaginative in their approach				
2b	New ideas are welcome in this firm				
2c	Innovative people are valued and rewarded here				
2d	People generally risk sharing their ideas because they are listened to and encouraged				
2e	Good ideas are quickly adopted by the firm				
3	**Power and conflict orientation**				
3a	There is an atmosphere of trust in this office				

No.	Orientation and culture	Definitely true	Mostly true	Mostly false	Definitely false
3b	There is a lot of criticism of procedures and working practices				
3c	People here tend to manipulate situations for their own personal advantage				
3d	There are cliques here who tend to look after themselves				
3e	Internal politics are a way of life for some people in the firm				
4	**Learning orientation**				
4a	When errors occur, the issues are discussed and learning takes place				
4b	Firm systems and procedures generally encourage learning in the first place				
4c	When a department learns something that is of value to other departments, this learning is quickly communicated				
4d	People here are too busy to work effectively				
4e	Partners here value a 'doing' rather than a 'learning' orientation among staff				
5	**Cooperation orientation**				
5a	People here are generally helpful and considerate of others				
5b	Most people here are good team players				
5c	People who work well in teams are usually rewarded				
5d	'Lend a helping hand' is a good description of how this firm works				

No.	Orientation and culture	Definitely true	Mostly true	Mostly false	Definitely false
5e	Everyone here has a strong sense of being a member of the firm				
6	**Trust orientation**				
6a	People here are generally trusting of others in the firm				
6b	People here do not attempt to exploit others				
6c	People here respect each other				
6d	People here do not take credit for the work accomplished by others				
6e	The firm is committed to its staff				
7	**Conflict orientation**				
7a	There are a lot of petty conflicts here				
7b	Departments tend to work together without rivalry				
7c	Criticism is taken as a personal affront in this firm				
7d	People here are always trying to win an argument				
7e	Conflict in this firm is generally more positive than negative				
8	**Future orientation**				
8a	People here think and plan ahead				
8b	Most people here are more interested in what will happen tomorrow rather than what happened yesterday				
8c	The firm's plans for the future are well known by everyone in the firm				

No.	Orientation and culture	Definitely true	Mostly true	Mostly false	Definitely false
8d	People here know their role in the firm's plans for the future				
8e	People are appraised and valued in terms of their future potential				
9	**Client service orientation**				
9a	The firm is focused on providing services to certain client markets				
9b	The partners demonstrate excellent service to clients at all times				
9c	People receive training on what our clients want from our service				
9d	People are encouraged to use their initiative in meeting clients' needs				
9e	People talk about clients in disparaging tones				

Source: Adapted from A. Brown (1998) *Organisational Culture*, Pearson Education Limited
© Andrew Brown 1995, 1998

11

Motivating your people to accept change

- For future success, firms must develop their people
- The importance of the influence of the team leader/department head on those within the team
- Overcoming resistance to change
- People need to understand why change is necessary and to feel involved in it
- The importance of letting people know what the firm's plans are and where they individually fit into them
- Training that is linked to the firm's business plan and to appraisals is essential to success

Change is about people

A successful firm values and cares for both its clients and its staff – success is derived from satisfied clients whose satisfaction has been generated by motivated people. Although to a client a fee earner is effectively 'the firm's service', everyone in a firm has a role to play in supporting and enabling that fee earner to provide the type and level of service that the client considers excellent. Thus the strength of a firm lies in the joint capabilities of all its members. In Chapter 10, we looked at how firms can create a positive climate for performance to enable client service to flourish. This chapter looks at how to motivate everyone in a firm to embrace that ethos and to become an effective team of people committed to delivering value both to clients and to the firm. Driven change, although easier to organise and more effective in the short term, only lasts as long as it is being pushed. Change is about people. Obtaining their commitment will involve their acceptance not only of the change itself, but of the values that lie behind it. The outcome should be something for which they themselves feel responsible, over which they have personal control, and in which they have confidence. What should always be remembered is that most people are motivated by a sense of being involved, a sense of understanding and a sense of purpose.

The process to achieve this will have to be consultative, participative and educative. To be consultative requires channels of communication; to be participative needs involvement; to be educative involves training. Once the change has been effected, the message will need consistent endorsement by partners and those in a position of leadership through-out the firm. Fee earners and staff will respond to fresh ideas far more pos-itively if a firm has enlightened people-management policies that are implemented fairly and consistently. The issues involved in to effective people development are summarised in Figure 11.1. You need targets and time recording, but legal firms are people organisations and, to prosper, your staff must be cared for and developed as people.

Building teams

Successful firms are skilfully led, and, in larger firms, this means at various levels in the firm as well as from the top. Research undertaken on behalf of the Chartered Institute of Personnel and Development[1] found that those closest to employees on a day-to-day basis have the greatest influ-ence on their attitude to work. In fact, top-down communication from senior management was generally seen as the least effective approach to getting key messages across. Employees' commitment to their work reflects the contacts they have with their line manager about their job, and the way in which their personal objectives and goals are set. Thus, when it comes to motivation, leadership is the function not of the senior partners alone, but of all individuals who have a working relationship with another person, such as department head or team leader, or even a person without significant management responsibility – a fee earner has a working relationship with his or her secretary. Similarly, David Maister, reporting on the results of an extensive survey of service industries,[2] found that success comes not from partners imposing a 'partnership line' but from individual leaders within the firm using their interpersonal skills to energise and enthuse those who work with them. If a department head or team leader is negative about change or implementing new working practices, there is little chance of the change being implemented. Regard-less of size of firm, careful thought needs to be given to the design of organisational structures and lines of communication to disseminate the desired message down from the firm's senior management to the teams and within them.

Teams play an important role in successful firms who take active steps to build them. Successful teams can operate with up to 20 people (including support staff) but other firms advocate that 15 active members are enough. Some larger firms base teams around specific clients, but in

---

Effective people development is concerned with:

Behaviour rather than **personality** – you can try to change a person's behaviour but you cannot change their personality or character. Therefore avoid commenting about them

Information rather than **belief** – base all comments on well-researched facts and not on the basis of surmised opinion. Opinions can be biased

Change rather than **evaluation** – although it is necessary to review progress, it is more important to make the requisite changes than beating about the bush and being overanalytical

Precision rather than **generalities** – people need precise information about what they should be learning. Telling people in general terms that their behaviour could be improved, but without informing them precisely what clients do not like about their current behaviour and giving them specific guidance as to how to change it, will not improve anything. In fact it is likely to have the opposite effect in that the behaviour will not change and the person will lose confidence and become demotivated. Nor is it sufficient to be told that a piece of work is good when the person is striving to be excellent. That person needs feedback on what would have made the difference between good and excellent, with an example if possible

Commitment rather than **compliance** – driven change will only result in compliance. You need commitment to change for it to be sustained.

Figure 11.1 Effective people development

Source: Adapted from G. Randell (1989) *Performance Appraisal in Human Resource Management*, Molander C. (ed.), Chartwell-Bratt

most practices they are work type based. In addition to the firm's overall business plan, each team or department should have its own business plan for the forthcoming year with clear objectives and each individual within that team should be aware of the part they play in achieving those objectives.

In many cases, department heads or team leaders will be partners but it should not be an automatic choice. Because solicitors usually come to management or supervisory roles without any formal management training, team leaders vary in their effectiveness. Solicitors and their staff are usually committed to their work, but lawyers tend to be extremely busy people who qualified to practise and not all see their role as managers or developers of their people – it is not 'their job'. Motivating a team of people in addition to managing relationships with clients is a new concept for many. Some people have a natural aptitude at being interested in and developing others while others lack confidence in their ability. Here, coaching and guidance can help them to become effective leaders. Coaching is a useful tool to help people achieve their potential, particularly with regard to developing skills such as facilitating meetings or the interpersonal competencies required in developing others. Mentoring from more senior partners, from someone with experience, can also be helpful. A few are just not 'people' minded and are better left to fee-earning work, including partners.

The saying 'do as I say and not as I do' is often the reality in legal firms. Because leaders play such a vital part in acting as role models, their good behaviour modelling should include:

- acting in a way that visibly supports the firm's stated values and objectives;
- actually delivering excellent service to clients;
- acting in a way that communicates high personal standards of performance;
- showing respect for those with whom you work;
- taking time to communicate effectively with others, allowing both parties to be honest about needs, issues, aspirations, ideas for change;
- demonstrating a sense of personal urgency and energy to achieve results;
- demonstrating a willingness to take decisions that may be unpopular or involve some personal risk.

The former Industrial Society's (now the Work Foundation) guide set out in Figure 11.2 provides useful principles and a helpful starting point for the effective management of a team.

Overcoming resistance to change

The greatest resistance to change may come from those at the top of the firm. Most partners in positions of seniority have a feeling of ownership of their client base. They are also usually self-confident, articulate, dominant, and convinced of the righteousness of their belief that they look after their own clients well and know whether they are happy with the service they receive. Their assumption may be correct, but it is invariably an assumption based on their views and not those of their clients. Despite the obvious advantages of having such personalities within a firm, there are potential dangers. Solicitors are used to giving advice to clients and to having what they say accepted as correct. Some may be unwilling to listen to advice, to work in teams, to collaborate with others, for example in passing work over, or to recognise their own weaknesses. Quite unknowingly they can foster a culture that hinders change. Others may view the adaptation of a more commercial approach as a slight on their 'professionalism' and the core values they perceive as forming the service they give to clients. Listening to clients and delivering a service they value will not bring about any reduction in ethical standards. Regardless of size of firm, partners must be convinced that innovation is the best

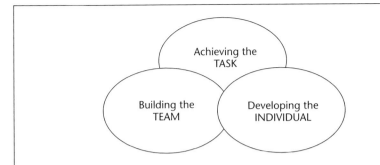

1. Set the task for the team; put it across with enthusiasm and remind people often
2. Make leaders accountable for 4–15 people; train them in leadership actions
3. Plan the work, check its progress, design jobs and arrange work to encourage the commitment of individuals in the team
4. Set individual targets after consulting; discuss progress with each person regularly and appraise at least once a year
5. Delegate decisions to individuals; if not, consult those affected by the decision
6. Communicate the importance of each person's job; support and explain decisions to help people apply them; brief team together monthly to monitor progress, policy, people and points for action
7. Train and develop all staff, especially the young; practise equal opportunities; gain support for the rules and procedures, set an example and 'have a go' at those that break them
8. Serve people in the team and care for their well-being and safety; work alongside people; deal with grievances promptly; attend social functions
9. Monitor action; learn from successes and mistakes; regularly walk round each person's place of work, observe, listen and praise

Figure 11.2   The Industrial Society's guide to good people management within teams

way to secure future growth and that complacency will kill it. Short-term efficiency improvements and working harder will only result in the work–life balance becoming even more uneven. Thus the first challenge may be to change the mindsets and attitudes of partners to persuade them to adopt an outward, client-oriented focus and to review their habitual ways of working. Various factors may act as a catalyst for focusing their minds on the need for change – falling profitability, the personality of the managing partner, an external event. Several partners may remain diehard for some time after the process of change has begun, in which case their negative impact must be minimised wherever possible.

Most people are naturally fearful of change if they feel that their present or future positions are threatened. It is up to the partners, heads of department and team leaders to recognise and overcome insecurity and uncertainty and to gain trust by involving those concerned in carefully planning changes and considering how they will affect those working with them. You are dealing with individuals, each of whom has greater or lesser degrees of ambition, fear, frustration, confidence, ability and resentment. Fears can develop for a variety of reasons. Everyone has their own perception of how a firm works and their role within it. People develop ways of working and doing routine tasks in certain ways, which to them are completely logical and reasonable. They are also familiar ways, and different people need varying levels of familiarity and security in their environment. Unless the reasons behind planned changes are fully explained and understood, those changes can meet with resistance. Changes in rewards structures, for instance, are usually seen as particularly threatening and will therefore be unpopular, as will any perceived diminution in personal status or esteem for an individual.

There has to be a process of education, at various levels, to obtain everyone's understanding of the need for change for the benefit to the firm overall. There will be a far greater readiness to accept change if partners and staff understand why it needs to happen and what the likely benefits will be. Trust in both the process and the outcome of change may need reinforcing on an individual level and is likely to involve:

- involvement and communication;
- career planning;
- training;
- establishing loyalty to the new values.

In many cases, the people concerned may have behaved and worked in the same way for years and are unlikely even to see the need for change. Those that are typecast as being resistant to change rarely see themselves in that light. The first step is to 'unfreeze' their mindset so that they become aware of the reasons for, and benefits of, change and are reassured about their own position. The way forward and who undertakes this task will depend on the individual's position and role in the firm but may involve a lot of tact, an understanding of the perceived problem, identifying and agreeing a solution with the person concerned and then actually implementing that solution. They will then need reassurance and confidence building to ensure that they accept the change.

A word of caution: beware of change for change's sake. A firm is a living system that needs internal checks and balances to keep it on a straight path. Listen to resistance to change and consider carefully what should be conserved and what changed.

Involvement and communication

People need to feel a sense of belonging. They need to feel confident that the firm's leaders know where it is going and that they can play an active role in achieving the firm's ambitions. Above all, they want to enjoy work and to look forward to a Monday morning. Effective consultation is built on good relationships and trust. Consulting employees, involving them and communicating with them all help to create a sense of trust and openness and to enhance commitment and motivation. Some firms may have to work harder at this than others. It may take time for people's scepticism as to whether a leopard can change its spots to dissipate in a practice in which financial targets have been the only issue on the agenda in the past. Similarly, a history of broken promises on the part of the firm or a perception of job insecurity will take time to overcome.

Transparency and involving everyone in the firm is the key to overcoming resistance to change and to gaining commitment. Let everyone know of the values that form the foundation of the firm, your aims for it and plans for achieving those aims. They should be made aware not only of plans for the firm as a whole but also of departmental plans and their own roles in making things happen which will have far greater relevance to them. It is natural for a person to feel more comfortable as a large fish in a small pond than a small fish in a large one. Thus a person can relate far more to the part they have to play in making their department or team achieve its objectives than to their part in the firm overall. A sense of insecurity or uncertainty is a great demotivator and so it is important to keep everyone informed of progress throughout the process of change by giving them regular updates on what has been achieved and what the next stage will be. Thank them for their involvement and contributions. Give them feedback on the firm's progress in achieving its objectives and on their role in it doing so. Give praise and recognition of their efforts, not only when change is accomplished but at stages on the way. Show that you appreciate the competence and skills of the person. Above all, remain positive and work on getting rid of feelings of insecurity and uncertainty.

How you keep people informed depends on the size of firm. Some larger firms hold an AGM backed up by quarterly reports to give information about what has been done and what is to happen. Further information can be drip-fed through an internal newsletter to ensure that the right messages are received. An annual meeting can be useful for firms of all sizes, including sole practitioners, because it acts as a discipline actually to tell staff of the firm's plans.

Ensure that regular meetings between staff and partners or team leaders take place after an initial meeting. These subsequent meetings should have a clear agenda that provides the opportunity for two-way feedback. Comments and questions should be encouraged – partners are not the sole instigators of good ideas. Share frustrations about problems within the current culture, for example secretaries complaining about fee earners not returning calls or their backlog of typing. Ask your staff to suggest ways of improving working practices, to suit clients not themselves. Look at existing practices and working habits and experiment with new ones.

Give greater responsibility and therefore ownership of working practices. Let everyone have an opportunity to experience positive feelings about the new culture. Allow people to commit themselves towards the new objectives; let them know where they fit in, what they have to do, how it is going to improve matters and their own working experience. However, bear in mind that if the firm's management and partners appear closed and uncommunicative, staff are likely to find it difficult to express their views and to make suggestions for improvements.

The way in which a firm instigates regular meetings will depend not only on its resources but also on the personalities involved. Larger firms usually hold regular departmental or team meetings. In some smaller practices, monthly lunchtime meetings with sandwiches can work well. In others, the clash of personalities is such that the meetings prove non-productive. One personality can adversely dominate a small group of people, in which case it may be helpful to work on that individual separately to ensure that he or she is 'on side' and that the individual's influence is used constructively. Take care to ensure that all meetings have a purpose and that staff do not feel that they are having to attend too many with the result that the purpose of them loses credibility. Avoid bureaucratic committees to ensure that flexibility is retained.

Partners and management teams must be accessible and approachable, not only so that staff will be willing to suggest ideas but they must also feel able to come forward about their concerns. Arranging informal social functions to which all staff are invited will create a greater feeling of cohesion within the firm and can help to break down barriers between different offices or departments. These events need not necessarily be lavish or costly, but it is important that partners attend. A drink after work each month helps in all firms. In larger firms, encourage different departments to organise and act as host. It is important that the various departments in a firm meet together to avoid a 'silo' culture (see Chapter 10 and Figure 10.3, pp. 103–4).

So often communication about the future of a firm is made in a cursory manner with little attempt to involve staff in any meaningful discussion. It is also inconsistent in many firms. Staff may be informed at the outset but then news of the firm's plans mysteriously dries up and they hear nothing further. Some managers consider that their staff are not interested in what is going on in the firm and that they only want to come in, work, be paid and go home, but they tend to be the poor communicators and motivators. In successful firms, staff feel part of the firm's plans for its future and embrace change because they understand where it is taking them. However, there has to be a balance between too little and too much communication can mean that staff are swamped with information and become confused. Information should be prioritised and filtered down according to the audience so that each member of a firm understands 'the big picture' and the smaller picture into which they fit.

Obtaining internal views

Surveys among staff and partners to gather everyone's views are the source of a great deal of useful information and assist in making everyone feel involved, provided that their views are taken into account.

- What do they consider are the strengths of the practice?
- What are the areas of weakness that would benefit from change/ development?
- How good is the firm at giving clients excellent service?
- Where could you improve?

Invite suggestions for improvements, and *use* the information. Ensure that you analyse the responses and collate the information promptly. Give feedback on all ideas – explain why they are either feasible or not feasible and if not, why not. Where possible, implement suggestions immediately and acknowledge who made them. If you do not show staff that their efforts are valued, they will soon stop trying.

Training

Training, development and learning will enhance capabilities, competencies and skills. They will lead to a more productive use of the firm's resources and to a more reliable service for clients. For individuals, they will provide greater fulfilment, self-esteem and job satisfaction and a consequent increase in individual motivation and morale in the firm overall. A firm's annual training programme should be based on the needs of the firm, departments and individuals but it should be in accordance with the firm's and departments' business plans. Training should be linked to a firm's appraisal system to ensure that individuals are being developed to their full potential. It should not be overlooked or postponed. Staff costs are one of your largest overheads and they should be developed as a resource for the benefit of the firm. It is short-sighted to cut down on training in an economic downturn; a well-trained staff is better motivated to understand a firm's objectives and will help it remain competitive. Melissa Hardee, chairman of the Legal Education and Training Group and training partner at CMS Cameron McKenna considers that staff want to be trained and to believe that their firm will help them to develop their potential.[3] Firms that develop their staff retain their staff. David Body,[4] partner in charge of Irwin Mitchell's

personal injury department believes that 'everyone from the most junior to the most senior should have the opportunity to do something
new to develop and enhance their career'.

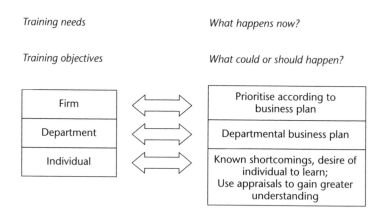

Figure 11.3 Training needs

Adopting a client service orientation will involve a variety of training.
We have seen that training or coaching in personal development skills
may be needed for successful teamworking. Training on the nature of the
solicitor–client relationship, the role of everyone in the firm in supporting and enabling that relationship, and the need to consider clients' perceptions of service is a useful starting point for any firm to effect the
change. Use the firm's research, and in particular the views of your clients
to establish other training needs. These views need to be collated and any
gaps in service delivery identified. The action to be taken and consequent
training will emerge from this information, from an internal survey, from
talking to professional referrers and from analysing the firm's record of
complaints. A variety of issues can cause perceptions of poor service
although the majority are communication and therefore behaviour
based. Poor responsiveness for instance can have one or more of several
causes: a fee earner who does not appreciate the client's need for information, poor management of the output of typing, inadequate use of IT,
poor time management, or overwork, for example. The actual cause will
have to be ascertained and appropriate remedies, including the requisite
training, found.

Most people benefit from time-management training. It helps individuals consider their personal goals and understand the concept of planning and prioritising a working day effectively. Clients do not understand
the need for solicitors to work excessively long hours; in fact, they see it
as a sign of inefficiency. That is not to deny that there are times when
there is no alternative, but working excessively long hours should not be

on an ongoing basis. However, saying that to one of the many over-worked and permanently tired solicitors who are unable to visualise any improvement in their position will bring a sharp response. Yet many of them do not plan their day or prioritise what is urgent and important. They fire-fight constantly and go from crisis to crisis, with the result that their level of service suffers and they blame their clients for constantly harassing them. Yet if they analysed their working day, delegated and made time for supervision, the work would be processed far more effectively and speedily with a happier client who will not resent paying a reasonable fee. It can take courage to take on another fee earner but with careful planning, delegation and supervision, profits will not go down.

Not all solicitors are good delegators, either of work or of administrative tasks. The right support staff with appropriate training can perform numerous back- and front-room tasks to process a matter more speedily. Work needs to be analysed to see which tasks can be performed by another person, and then the requisite training and supervision given. The reason that it is quicker for the fee earner to do the task him or herself is invariably an excuse for failing to organise the workload. Commercial lawyers are more familiar with working in teams than private client practitioners. Administration is frequently confused with management whereas the former can often be delegated. Partners complain that they have no time to manage their practice, but the tasks that occupy their time frequently relate to administration, tasks that could be delegated to someone with the requisite skill thereby relieving the partner to concentrate on actual management or fee-earning work. Most firms have support staff who would make extremely good administrators with training. Many will be reticent about their ability to perform new tasks and to expand their capabilities but, with encouragement and support, they can become of even greater value to a firm. It is often far less risky to train a person you know for a new role than to recruit someone who is an unknown quantity, however good your recruitment procedures.

A common failing in many firms is inadequate training for their IT systems. Practices invest thousands of pounds in their systems but baulk at training costs and consequently do not get the full benefit of their investment. This has a knock-on effect on client service because the more efficient working processes do not materialise and the overwork and consequent delays continue.

CHAPTER SUMMARY

1. Ensure appropriate organisational structures and channels of communication.

2. Establish an understanding of all the issues that are involved in sustaining any change.

3. Have the courage to pick the right person to be a department head/team leader.

4. People need to feel involved and to understand where they fit into the firm's plans.

5. Ensure fairness and consistency.

6. Do not swamp people with information. Let them know the firm's plans overall and filter down information that is relevant to them and their department.

7. Communication, communication, communication, including listening.

8. Training, training, training

Notes

1   Professor D. Guest and Dr N. Conway (2001) *Employer Perception of the Psychological Contract*, Chartered Institute of Personnel and Development.
2   D. Maister (2001) *Practice What You Preach: What Managers Must Do to Create a High Achievement Culture*, Free Press.
3   M. Hardee [2002] *Gazette*, 17 January.
4   L. Tsang, 'Typing pool to equity pool', [2001] *Gazette*, 18 January 32.

12

Financial management

- Firms must be able to interpret financial information and understand what it is telling them
- Firms need a sound understanding of their profitability and margins when offering alternative methods to hourly rate billing
- Profitability should be understood at various levels: firm, departmental and fee earner
- Firms should also understand the profitability of work types and of individual clients

Financial management and client service

Financial information may seem a strange bedfellow of excellent client service, but it plays an important part in enabling a firm to provide the desired service in two respects. In the first place, financial information, and a sound interpretation and understanding of it, forms the basis of some of the decision making referred to in Chapter 9 when a firm is identifying which markets are profitable and, taking into account other external factors and value to the client, how to design each service to give value to clients and maintain levels of profitability.

Secondly, financial management is required to achieve the balance between the needs of the client in the form of the reduction of perceived risk and value for money and those of the firm to generate sufficient income to cover overheads and working capital, and a level of profit for partners. The relationship between profitability and alternative methods of billing can be complex and you need a thorough understanding of the firm's financial standing and profitability before you can offer different fee arrangements to clients. How often when you accept instructions do you know whether the fee you are likely to be able to charge will make you a profit? Are you aware of the actual cost of producing the work and the margins involved? Nick Jarrett-Kerr,[1] former chief executive of Bevan Ashford, identified that the better partners can come to understand financial issues, the better the firm seems to perform. However, two problems face the financial managers of many firms:

1. Partners often do not understand the firm's accounts or the way in which the firm funds its business.
2. Partners do not like to admit their lack of knowledge.

This chapter does not aim to cover all areas of financial management, but summarises aspects of it that are required to enable a firm to meet client needs.

Management accounts

Management accounts should be distinguished from the firm's annual accounts that provide historical information and, although useful to compare from year to year and for some benchmarking purposes, do not provide the requisite data with which to run a business. Management accounting information enables you to:

- understand where your firm is now;
- decide on your future direction;
- monitor whether you are on track;
- highlight any potential problems;
- achieve your objectives.

As a useful starting point to assess your firm's financial management skills, respond to the questions in Table 12.1 as objectively as you can.

The format of management accounts

Most computerised systems will produce numerous reports, but unless these are interpreted and the implications of the figures understood, they are of little value. Their volume is often overwhelming for busy fee earners. Instead, present the information they need on an A4 sheet that gives only the essential figures. Summarising the information may involve extricating key figures and entering them on an Excel spreadsheet to produce the requisite simple format and/or tables that show trends in figures over time – looking at figures in isolation will not necessarily give meaningful information. All reports should be in a clear and simple format with figures rounded up or down. Lawyers tend to be overanalytical and to become bogged down in detail whereas you should be looking for the bigger picture: what are the trends, what do these figures tell us, what action do we need to take? You can always revert to the full report for greater detail if necessary. By comparing figures over time and by using

Table 12.1   Financial management assessment

Please score your own firm against the following criteria (on a scale from 7 (excellent) to 1 (poor))

	Excellent		Good		OK		Poor
	7	6	5	4	3	2	1
We have a strong market focus							
We can accurately assess the profitability of both overall client market and individual clients within that market							
We monitor the profitability of each client market over time							
We can accurately assess the profitability of each work type by department and individual fee earner							
Our overheads allow us to be competitive in the client markets we serve							
Our management accounts are in simple format that is understandable by all our partners							
All our fee earners record time efficiently and accurately							
We are aware of the profitability of different types of fee arrangement							
Our knowledge when we accept instructions of whether the fee we are likely to be able to charge will make us a profit							
We usually have the right level of fee earner carrying out work to ensure that it is profitable							
Our fee earners have the optimum number of files for them to manage effectively							

percentages you can build up a view of what is happening to the firm overall and in each department.

Time recording

Time recording forms the basis of management accounting because it forms a record of your stock in trade. Your management accounts will be of far less value, if not meaningless, without accurate time recording. How do you know whether any work has been profitable if you do not know how much it has cost you to produce it? Some practitioners do not see the need to record time on matters for which a fixed fee is charged, residential conveyancing for example, but it is essential to monitor the profitability of work and whether the margins you are achieving can be improved without detriment to the level of service. Fee earners *must* understand the importance of time recording and be encouraged to record time fully. They must also recognise the need for accuracy and be discouraged from padding time. Irrecoverable time should be written off as soon as a bill in respect of the work has been delivered. In conveyancing, write-offs should take place on the conclusion of a matter.

Set reasonable targets that take the nature of the work into account. It is far easier to record a full eight hours doing commercial work for a single client than in respect of numerous matters for private clients, even though the fee earner doing the latter may have been fully occupied all day. Targets for time vary across firms but many consider that to achieve five and a half chargeable hours in a day, which equates to 1,265 in a year if a fee earner works 46 weeks a year, is reasonable. Recording non-chargeable time is also extremely useful, providing care is taken to provide relevant codes, such as research, supervision or management. It is important to evaluate the value to the firm of non-chargeable time periodically but do not take too short term an approach. Just because something cannot be measured in hard financial terms immediately does not mean that it will not have significant value in the longer term. It is essential to recognise the time that it takes to manage a firm to achieve success.

In some firms, standard costing for work of a highly routine nature that is undertaken by junior fee earners has taken the place of time recording. Such firms have sophisticated financial management and a thorough understanding of their cost base. For the majority of firms and work types, time recording remains the only reliable means of understanding the cost of producing work.

Opening files

Accuracy is also required when opening files. Merely opening a file takes time and is therefore a cost to the firm, so get it right. Matter types on the firm's computer system should be sufficiently wide to provide meaningful information but not so wide as to make it a farce. They should be looked at on an annual basis to ensure that they still reflect the work types that the firm undertakes, or intends to undertake as part of its business plan. It is a useful check to see that the firm is still on focus and that work outside the planned markets is not being undertaken, or if it is, whether there are any new areas that the firm should be considering. Again, fee earners and support staff should be given training on the importance of correctly identifying the nature of work at the outset, and of notifying the cashier's department of any requisite changes as a matter progresses.

Profitability

Most partners and fee earners have had little training to understand the implications of the figures in management accounts, the 'so what' factor, and therefore many focus solely on fee income without looking at the profitability of that income. They frequently forget that clients are the main drivers of profit. Work has to be undertaken with the appropriate mix of fee earners and resources to give value and perceived value for money to clients. Fees will be determined by the price sensitivity of the work.

Profitability is dependent not just on a firm's overheads but on how it uses its resources, in particular:

- the number of fee earners to equity partners;
- the direct costs of producing the work (the cost of fee earners, including partners, and secretarial staff involved in producing the work) – the gross profitability margin;
- the amount of chargeable time fee earners record;
- how much of that time is actually billed and recovered;
- non-salary overheads;
- the cost of working capital.

Profitability should be understood at various levels as shown in Figure 12.1.

Firm, office and departmental profitability

The gross profitability of the firm, and of offices or departments/teams within it can be calculated on a quarterly basis and the gross profitability percentages compared across time. It is an indicator of performance and a fairer way of comparison than fee income alone because it takes account of the cost of producing the work. For instance, it is frequently

Figure 12.1   The profitability triangle

assumed that commercial work is the most profitable because it usually generates the highest fee income but the cost of the more expensive fee earners required to produce it can result in it being less profitable than other departments. The higher fees may of course mean that it still makes a greater contribution to profits overall. Leaving comparisons at department level encourages a team-based culture rather than lauding the highest earning individual fee earners.

To calculate a gross profitability:

Total fee income (less any write-offs) − Direct costs = Gross profit

Direct costs are the fee earners' salaries and a notional salary for partners engaged in providing the service plus the salaries of secretarial staff. At the time of publication the Law Society suggests a notional salary of £31,500 for partners outside London and £41,450 within London. However, those figures were set some time ago and a more realistic figure is the cost of a senior fee earner to undertake the relevant type of work. If a fee earner does more than one type of work, apportion the salary according to the proportion of their total fees from each type. If an expensive case management system has been introduced in lieu of secretarial staff in any department, it may be fairer to include that cost in the calculations as well. Allocating and deducting further costs makes the process overly complicated at this stage, unless it would be grossly unfair not to do so; if, for example, if accommodation costs for one office were significantly higher than those of another.

Calculate the percentage of gross profit to income and consider it across different work types.

Gross profitability percentage

$$\frac{Gross\ profit}{Fee\ income} \times 100$$

Remember to keep all the calculations simple – do not get hung up trying to overanalyse. You want a simple, objective view. Using a table, such as Table 12.2, gives a broader picture of any trends.

Some firms achieve gross profitability of 55–60 per cent across all departments.[2] Such firms have good management, organisational structures specifically tailored to the services offered and segments of client markets served, and ensure that the right level of fee earner undertakes the work with the appropriate level of IT and/or secretarial support.

Although each of the following figures should be looked at on a monthly basis for the firm overall and for each department, they should also be compared over time. Putting each in a simple table or using bar

Table 12.2   Gross profitability percentage comparisons

	Commercial	Residential conveyancing	Probate	Family	Litigation/PI	Firm
	%	%	%	%	%	%
Quarter 1						
Quarter 2						
Quarter 3						
Quarter 4						
Overall						

charts or graphs emphasises any trends or areas in which management needs strengthening:

- work in progress;
- time recorded;
- bills delivered.

Fee earner profitability

Department heads or team leaders should review on a monthly basis figures for all fee earners within their department/team, consider the implications and, on a management by exception basis, discuss problems and solutions with individual fee earners. Firms that have instigated systems of file review such as those required by Lexcel or Legal Services Commission contracts will already have this mechanism in place. Key figures to be considered should be:

- work in progress;
- time recorded;
- bills delivered;
- aged debt;
- outstanding disbursements;
- number of current files;
- number of new matters;
- date of last movement on any file if, for example, more than one month.

Calculating the actual hours recorded as a percentage of the desired target indicates the productivity of a fee earner, provided that account is also taken of any time subsequently written off. Comparing the respective hours recorded by individual fee earners within a department on a bar chart can demonstrate whether the team is working effectively. If a department head records the greatest number of fee-earning hours in the team but few non-chargeable hours, is that person delegating work and spending sufficient time managing and supervising?

Do fee earners have the optimum number of files? Too few will mean that they cannot make the requisite contribution to profit and too many that they cannot deal with them efficiently or effectively, which will result in client dissatisfaction and potential negligence claims. It is an area that is often overlooked with senior fee earners, until a problem arises.

The profitability of clients

It is important to know the contribution to profit and the profitability of work undertaken for the various types of client for whom you act. The following categories that you can adapt to fit your own client base were given in Chapter 7:

* high-value, individual key clients;
* key clients;
* general clients;
* low-value, high-volume clients.

You should calculate the percentage of your work that comes from individual clients or each category of client, in terms of both fee income and its profitability, by taking into account not only the cost of the resources involved in producing the work but also any relevant money costs associated with its production or lock-up of work in progress, outstanding costs or disbursements.

Recovery rates, money costs and lock-up

Money costs money and the cost of the provision of working capital should be taken into account when considering the profitability of departments or work types, or work for individual clients. This is particularly relevant to PI and publicly funded work where not only the cost of the work has to be carried but in the case of the former, disbursements often remain outstanding for long periods as well. The following is one way of calculating the cost to the firm:

WIP + Outstanding fees + disbursements
$$\times$$
Percentage rate of interest on bank loans and overdrafts

Fee earners must understand that doing the work alone will not pay their salaries. WIP has to be recorded and then converted not only into bills but into paid bills so that the value of those fees are not diminished and there are sufficient funds to pay the fee earners' salaries. The rate at which a firm, department or fee earner converts work in progress into bills should be taken into account.

$$\frac{Fees\ for\ a\ period}{WIP\ to\ period} \times 365 \qquad = Number\ of\ days$$

Similarly, firms can compare how quickly bills are being collected in any period, at a firm, department or individual level, as follows:

$$\frac{Fees\ outstanding}{Cumulative\ fees\ rendered} \times 365 \qquad = Number\ of\ days\ outstanding$$

Again, make comparisons across departments and over time to assess trends.

Recovery rates in terms of write-offs of bills or work in progress can also impact on profitability and working capital requirements. These can be calculated for the firm overall and for individual offices and departments/teams. If there is a problem, the rates for individual fee earners can be investigated. To calculate the percentage of WIP that is actually converted into bills in any period:

$$\frac{Write\text{-}offs}{WIP} \times 100$$

Aged debt needs careful management to ensure that it does not adversely affect the profitability of work. It should be minimised if financial agreements are made with clients at the outset, and adhered to throughout a matter but we are not in a perfect world and every firm should have an effective credit control system. Increasing numbers of firms send statements because many clients expect them and only pay when they receive one. For that reason, statements should be sent out before the expiration of the time allowed for payment.

Responsibility for collection should be clearly allocated. In some firms, cashiers undertake debt collection while in others it remains the responsibility of the individual fee earner. Neither is usually totally satisfactory because cashiers are generally too busy to be involved with debt collection and do not prioritise it and a busy fee earner will often put off chasing a client for fear of upsetting them. It is therefore usually cost-effective for firms of all sizes to employ a credit controller, on a part-time basis if necessary. An individual with a pleasant client manner who systematically chases debts by phone call and/or letter should soon prove cost-effective. Fee earners should rarely be allowed to put a stop on chasing payment. Does the firm really want clients who are bad payers?

Overheads

Reviewing all overheads other than salary costs as a percentage of gross fees and comparing that percentage across time and with that of other firms is another useful indicator. Overheads are all expenses involved in running the office other than those included in the gross profitability calculation, such as accommodation costs, salary costs of a cashier's department and receptionist, training and IT. A good level to aim for is 30 per cent of fee income.[3] Firms should remember that cutting overheads will not necessarily increase profitability in times of crisis. You should always seek good value and not adopt too short term an approach, by forsaking training when times are difficult for instance.

The following ratio assesses what is happening to all the overheads of the practice.

$$\frac{Net\ profit\ before\ tax}{Fees} \times 100$$

The resulting percentage tells you what it costs you to produce every £100 of fee income, a useful comparison to make over time.

The profitability of a matter: an effective pricing strategy

Offering the lowest quote may secure work, but do you want it? Can you afford to do it? Firms argue that they have to undertake some work as a 'loss leader' but rarely evaluate whether subsequent work is sufficiently profitable to cover both. An effective pricing strategy is based on:

- the value of your service to your client;
- your costs of production;
- your charge-out rates;
- the effects of alternative methods of billing on your profitability.

Remember that price and value do not equate to the same thing to your clients who want an alternative to hourly rate billing, but offering fixed prices and estimates involves you being aware of your own margins. Even if an hourly rate has to be charged, firms base the rate they offer on 'the going rate' for the work type in their location, without considering the segment of the market they are aiming at and regardless of what it is actually costing them to produce that work. Market forces may dictate the price you can charge, particularly for 'commodity' type work, but to charge, for example, £95.00 per hour when one of your competitors charges £105.00 and another £85.00 does not distinguish you from either of them. Instead consider the segment of the market you are aiming for and how price sensitive it is, and then consider your costs of production. Do your overheads allow you to be competitive in markets in which you operate?

Creating efficient, profitable working structures for each service is essential to ensure profitability and the cost and productivity of the resources involved have to be taken into account. Depending on the position of the work on the value curve (see Chapter 9 and Figure 9.7, pp. 88–9) and its price sensitivity consider:

- What steps should you take to minimise your cost of production?
- What is the key limiting factor on profitability?
- How can you minimise it?
- Will working in teams using different levels of fee earner improve profitability? Will the use of a case management system improve productivity and reduce the need for support staff?
- Are you obtaining full value from your IT systems: should you arrange further training or adjust working practices?

Bear in mind that being busy does not equate to being profitable.

Firms should identify the factors that have the largest impact on their cost base. These are likely to be salaries, particularly in London where firms have had to reconsider working practices to minimise their cost. Some practices have moved to having no support staff but the impact of this on the quality of service given to clients should also be taken into account. The right balance between a fee earner's use of IT and secretarial support has to be struck for each work type. Accommodation costs usually have the second greatest impact and firms should consider these when planning which services to offer. For example, can Legal Services Commission-funded family work be profitable when conducted from expensive city centre offices?

Calculating hourly rates

Unless you understand your costs of production, you cannot price work effectively and you cannot make decisions as to how to improve profitability. Although hourly charge-out rates are routinely set for fee earners within most firms, it is only the minority that actually calculate how much it costs them to produce work each year. For most work types, the most effective way is to break down that cost to an hourly cost rate per fee earner.

All costs involved in the production of the service should be apportioned on either a use or a weighted basis according to fee earner or department and then divided by the number of hours that the fee earner will be expected to record as chargeable time. Some firms base their calculation on 80 per cent of that time to take account of write-offs. The Law Society has published useful guidelines.[4]

Understanding how to price work

To estimate and/or offer a fixed price involves knowing not only how much it costs to produce the service but also how many hours will be involved in that production. Many practitioners consider that they are good 'estimators' of the time taken to carry out work and therefore how to price it. They may be, but, until they have actually taken the following steps, they cannot say that with any degree of accuracy. Practitioners need to 'fillet' files, i.e. take them apart so that you can see their structure. You should look at both dead and current files and those of other fee earners undertaking the same sort of work and then consider the following.

- Identify the common key stages in the matter type.
- Segment each stage into tasks and related sub tasks.
- Using time printouts, what is the average time taken to complete each task and sub task?
- Does this vary with different fee earners?
- What resources do you need to complete each task in respect of fee earner hours, support staff hours, and specific matter costs such as photocopying?
- Estimate the time and cost of each resource.
- What is the likely variability of each resource and the time estimate across matters?
- What margin do you need to build into your fixed price or estimate to cover that variability?

This may seem a laborious task but it only has to be undertaken infrequently and, once completed, you will be able to price work with far greater certainty.

CHAPTER SUMMARY

1.   Partners must acknowledge that profitability is driven by the client markets that the firm serves, and the way in which the firm's services are designed.

2. Managers should take steps to ensure that partners understand and are able to interpret management accounting information and the implications of it.

3. Firms should concentrate not on fee income but on the profitability of that income.

4. Firms must understand the key factors of their cost base and their margins.

5. Firms should undertake accurate assessments of their costs of production on a regular basis.

Notes

1   N. Jarrett-Kerr, *Managing for Success*, Law Management Success, law management section July 2002.
2   Law Management Section, Law Society/BDO Stoy Hayward Financial Benchmarking Survey 2001.
3   Ibid.
4   Law Society (1992) *The Expense of Time*, Law Society Publishing.

13

Risk management: systems and procedures

- Risk management permeates all areas of practice management and must not be ignored
- Quality standards benefit firms and provide a framework for risk management
- Do not overfocus on systems and procedures – the attitudes of those operating them are more important
- Client needs should form the basis of systems and procedures which must also be perceived as credible by those operating them
- Effective supervision for all is vital for risk management
- First meetings are extremely important in understanding and managing client expectations

Risk management: a framework

> Performing the client's work as quickly and efficiently as possible with the minimum risk of a mistake being made.[1]

Legal matters are never identical, even in the most routine, commodity type of work. No two clients are the same and each will have different expectations of your service. Nor can you dictate how the interpersonal relationship between fee earner and client should be conducted. Thus legal services are a potential minefield of risk, in respect not only of potential negligence claims, but also of client complaints. What you can do is to train fee earners to understand client needs and to have systems and procedures in place that are used by a well-trained staff and backed up by an effective use of IT to enable fee earners to deliver a service that is both efficient and reliable and with the minimum exposure to the risk of a mistake being made. Firms should view risk management proactively; it is much cheaper to avoid having to deal with a complaint or to make a claim than to pay the consequences of making a mistake.

One person in a firm needs to take overall responsibility for risk management and, in view of the fact that it permeates all aspects of practice management, the most appropriate person will probably be the managing partner or chief executive, backed up by other members of the firm's management team. Their function should be to create firm-wide risk management policies, to evaluate their effectiveness periodically and to ensure that they cover all current risks. These will include (inter alia) policies relating to areas of practice management, undertakings, organisational structures and lines of communication, managing billing, recruitment, appraisals, IT knowledge and communication systems. Firms should monitor compliance with firm policies in branch offices. John Verry[2] suggests that you begin by considering the following underlying causes of claims to identify the risks to which your firm is exposed:

- missed time limits;
- delay;
- communication failure with clients and other professionals;
- inadequate delegation;
- lack of supervision;
- undertakings;
- poor organisation;
- poor practice management standards;
- lack of knowledge of the law.

Firms can obtain a copy of the Solicitors' Indemnity Fund self-assessment risk audit[3] to complete themselves to help identify practice areas where they are exposed to risk.

Quality standards

The Law Society Lexcel accreditation and CLSQM (the Community Legal Service Quality Mark) have been drafted to provide practice management standards that cover the main causes of complaint and claims brought against solicitors, most of which relate not to the quality of the advice itself but to poor service delivery. Specifically Lexcel relates to:

- management structure;
- services and forward planning;
- financial management;
- managing people;
- office administration;
- case management.

Firms report that Lexcel certification serves to enhance client relationships and promotes consistency and uniformity throughout the firm.[4] Similarly, the Investors in People (IIP) quality standard can act as a catalyst for firms to manage change. Those that have achieved IIP accreditation report a major improvement in profitability and staff satisfaction.[5] Further interest in Lexcel is likely to be generated on the introduction of rules in the next edition of *Guide to the Professional Conduct of Solicitors* that will require a practice to manage its business effectively.

Undermanagement and overmanagement: a balance

Poor systems result in an inefficient service to clients and a demotivated staff. On the other hand, firms can be overregulated and rely too heavily on systems and procedures, which can be equally demotivating. An overreliance on systems can stultify a person's instinct as to whether something is wrong, and blindly following the book does not promote initiative. Above all, the reason for carrying out the work, providing a service to clients, should not be overlooked. Firms should guard against focusing on internal quality for the sake of reducing insurance premiums at the cost of meeting clients' needs. All systems should be designed to deliver services to meet clients' needs and expectations or to understand and manage those expectations. Get your product right first and then design the systems so that you deliver it consistently, reliably and efficiently.

The Alexander Forbes risk management team found that systems and procedures themselves, while essential, are not the ultimate solution to risk management. What *does* make a difference is attitude to risk and an open culture in which everyone in a firm shares the desire to improve and to eliminate mistakes.[6] Firms with a culture of blame invite future trouble because staff will be reluctant to admit mistakes and consequent damage will not be limited. In some firms, employees are dismissed for making a mistake without any examination of the reason for it happening. In fact, the mistake may have been the result of poor management, an overload of work or inadequate supervision for example. Mistakes should be viewed constructively as a learning experience and training given or improvements implemented to prevent them recurring. Partners and department heads should always be seen to lead by example in observing systems and procedures. If they have a negative attitude towards them, there is little chance that members of their department will comply.

Systems and procedures that work

The success of systems and procedures in reducing errors totally depends on the credibility of the system and the consequent attitudes of the people using them. Systems have to be considered both to be relevant and to reflect the best way of working. What purpose a fat office manual that gathers dust on a library shelf? Some systems or procedures have to be firm wide and there also has to be an element of consistency across procedures used in individual departments, agreed between a firm's management and its department heads. Thereafter, short departmental manuals containing the systems and procedures that relate to the operation of a specific department and the management of the work of its clients will be of far greater relevance to the people using them. If people are asked to contribute to developing those procedures and for their suggestions on ways of improving working practices, those procedures are far more likely to be observed and mistakes minimised than had they been imposed from above. Psychologically, people feel it is their system and take ownership of it. Similarly, fee earners should be involved in designing IT case management and knowledge systems to avoid vital elements being omitted from programmes.

You may need to provide training for new procedures to ensure they are fully adopted. Listen to staff who use a system to learn whether further training would enable them to operate it more efficiently. New members of staff will require training on the firm's and departments' systems and procedures as part of their induction.

Departmental systems

In addition to assessing risk at a practice management level, firms should also consider potential risk for each work type that they undertake. This is best done at departmental or team level and each department or practice area should, under the management and supervision of the department head, also:

- identify the most common mistakes made by fee earners when carrying out their work;
- agree the cause of the mistake;
- agree the course of action every team member must take to eliminate the risk of the mistake occurring;
- design checklists and templates;
- circulate templates and share knowledge with other departments.

Departments should also regularly evaluate their procedures and review whether they should address any new or potential risks.

One of the most important aspects of risk management is a common system across a department for keeping and working on files, particularly if several fee earners work on the same matter or in the absence of the fee earner. Always keep attendance notes and a record of advice given.

All fee earners should be aware of risk management not only because of the potential financial cost to the firm but of the damage that client dissatisfaction does to the relationship with your client. Partners should encourage fee earners to talk about problem files by acknowledging that they too have files on which they have a mental block. Tackle such a file first thing in the morning, or ask someone else to have a look at it, just to get it moving again. If there are several, do one each day. Remember that a file is not completed while there are loose ends – including, for example, until the recovery of costs is concluded. It is easy not to continue to drive a file when the bulk of the work, and the most interesting part, is finished, but to a client the matter is still very much alive. They want their money. Where possible, fee earners should pass the file to someone who will concentrate on finishing the matter and will continue to keep the client informed.

Supervision

Lexcel and CLSQM office administration and case management provisions contain useful guidelines relating to supervision and file audit and keeping central diary systems.

Working in teams with varying levels of fee earner means not only that one person should be in overall control of the team but that there are more people to supervise. Management time should be allowed for supervision because it plays a vital role in managing the delivery of the service and in creating profitability. Effective supervision means managing the whole team's performance, including the performance of partners, and not just that of junior or inexperienced staff. Partners should lead by example and be prepared to have their work examined by another competent person. Partners or senior fee earners who are not supervised may become mavericks who dabble in areas in which they do not have expertise, or take on too much work and, as a consequence, incur claims. Supervisors should:

- monitor the nature of work fee earners undertake to make sure it is within their area of expertise and capability;
- ensure that all members of a team keep abreast of developments in the law that impact on their practice area.

Supervisors should be proactive. Regular file reviews are the most effective way of ensuring that potential problems are uncovered at an early stage and dealt with. A supervisor does not need to look at every file, merely a selection from which a picture of the standard of work can be seen. The number will depend on the capability of the fee earner. In addition to financial management issues, supervisors should review current workloads. Does a fee earner have too many or too few files? The former can be as detrimental to client service as the latter is to profitability. Taking on additional work in the absence of a colleague can also put too much strain on a fee earner with consequent risk management implications.

Many firms have central computer diary systems within the department or firm in addition to any system maintained by individual fee earners. It is essential that all fee earners use the systems. It is also essential that all information fed into systems is accurate: no matter how good your diary and review systems, they will be ineffective unless it is. Always double-check your calculations on deadlines and ask someone else to confirm them. Check diary entries made by support staff, because the fee earner will be responsible if they are wrong.

Delegation

Delegation should be dealt with in a structured manner. Files should not merely be 'dumped' on another fee earner. You should maintain responsibility for a file even if you have asked someone else to work on it. Make a diary note and put a note on the file of who is delegating and for what purpose, with timescales, and any deadlines. Summarise the background to the matter. In the case of junior fee earners, delegation should be made through the supervisor to ensure that the fee earner is not overwhelmed with work and that the individual has the expertise to undertake it. If you take over a file, do not assume that someone else's conclusions are right. Similarly, just because someone of repute has checked a title, do not assume it is right.

Fee earners should be trained to plan and prioritise work. Have periods during which you do not take phone calls to enable you to deal with more complicated work. Let clients know you will ring them back at a certain time, and do so. Manage interruptions by indicating in some way that you are not available for a period of time. Use to-do lists and work out what is important and urgent and must be done immediately.

- What steps need to be taken and by when?
- Have you made any assumptions?
- How can you check if they are correct?
- List all the points that need to be checked and cross them off when you have done so:

    - with your client;

- within the firm; or
- from an outside source.

Never assume what your client's instructions will be; always consult and involve them.

Managing clients' expectations

In Chapter 3 we saw how clients form expectations of legal services and that what each and every one of your clients expects from you will be different. Private clients in particular are not familiar with legal processes, or how you spend your day or run your office. Their hopes for the outcome of their matter may be wholly unachievable, despite what their mate in the pub told them. Remember that they will be approaching the service from a perspective totally different from your own. The matter will be extremely important to them, and they feel at risk and need information. They may have what you consider to be highly unreasonable expectations of what you can do for them, but to your clients, those expectations are quite reasonable. The only certain thing is that if you do not meet their expectations, your clients will be, at worst, dissatisfied and moan to their family and friends; at best, they will actually complain and at least give you the chance to put matters right.

You cannot assume that your clients know anything about legal processes, or that you are working on their behalf if you have not specifically informed them, or that they will realise that costs are accruing all the time. What is obvious to you is not obvious to your clients. Remember that you are in the driving seat and it is up to you to listen and understand what your clients want and to manage what they expect from you, from the outset.

Managing first meetings

The first meeting forms the foundation of both:

- the solicitor–client relationship; and
- the financial agreement with the firm.

Use checklists to ensure that all issues are dealt with at the first meeting. Each department should establish its own checklist of key points. You should also consider:

- Who is to see a new client for the first time?
- Can that person assess the potential of the work and how it should be costed?

First meetings are an opportunity to get to know the client. Always be aware of the anxiety and risk they may be feeling. No matter how short the time and how much pressure the client puts you under, always try to meet a new client in person. You cannot know a client on the basis of a phone call. Although you may consider it uneconomical, spend some time to find out what your client's expectations are; it will save money in the long run. Understand where your client is coming from, and explain in simple terms exactly what you can do for them and what level of service they can expect from you. Otherwise, the client will continue with unreasonable ideas, become dissatisfied and then it is too late. Be clear and do not fudge any issues. Misunderstandings arise because a fee earner has not used language with which the client is familiar, 'legal jargon' according to your client.

Always take full instructions – you need to understand what your client wants from the matter. However, always give realistic advice, even if this is contrary to your client's expressed hoped-for outcome, and point out fully the processes and procedures involved, and likely timescales. Explain, for instance, that there is no certainty in litigation. Let the client know whether he or she is likely to have to bear the burden of costs at the end of the day and to what extent they may be recoverable from the other side. Record verbal instructions on an attendance note and read them back to the client at the end of the meeting. Write to confirm to avoid subsequent confusion if need be.

- What do they want you to do?
- What timescales are involved?
- Do you have full details?
- Have you given them realistic advice?

Some points to consider

- Who is to deal with the matter?
- Which level of fee earner? Agree with the client who is to undertake the work and be specific about their status in the firm. Confirm that a junior fee earner will receive supervision and that a partner can always be contacted to discuss the file.
- Introduce them to the fee earner.

Billing

Information to be given to clients about costs was discussed in Chapter 6 on managing billing. The main points to consider are:

- What type of billing arrangement?
- How frequently are bills to be sent?

- If a fixed price or estimate, always specify the extent of the work that the price covers, and reserve the right to increase the fees after further consultation with the client if additional work is involved.
- How and when are disbursements to be paid?
- Clients need ongoing information about costs. Keep them informed of how costs are accumulating throughout the matter.
- Do not exceed an estimate without first going back to clients to obtain their further instructions.

Communication

- How are you going to communicate with clients?
- How frequently?
- By what means?
- Phoning clients to give them an update is not a waste of their money. Rather it is likely to be perceived as creating value by keeping them informed and involved.
- Use your diary system to ensure that you do communicate in accordance with the agreement.

Involving your client

- Outline the matter and agree how the matter is to proceed up to the first stage.
- Point out the level of uncertainty and risk and do a cost–benefit analysis with the client, if appropriate.
- Agree responsibilities.
- Confirm that you will involve the client in deciding how the matter is to proceed throughout.
- What will you have to do?
- What does your client have to do, which documents do they have to provide, when will they be needed?
- Use simple, straightforward language and give a clear explanation of any legal term.
- Does your client want to raise anything else?
- Is your client totally clear about what is to happen and in agreement with the course of action?
- Keep your client informed and involved at *all* stages of the matter.

Always send a confirmatory letter to clients, clearly identifying their instructions and specifying what you will do, and confirming what they must do. Set out timescales and explain about any limitation periods again. The Solicitors' Costs Information and Client Care Code 1999 also requires that you let your client know about whom to contact in the event of dissatisfaction. Many firms use the first letter to confirm financial arrangements but take care to avoid making it overly lengthy. See Chapter 6 on managing billing for suggested alternatives. Whichever method you choose, you must notify your client in writing of the financial agreement and request that he or she sign a copy. Always send a copy of the agreement if you have to renegotiate costs at a later date.

Accounting errors

In 2000, 17 per cent of the service complaints received by the Office for the Supervision of Solicitors (OSS) related to conveyancing and half of those arose from incorrect accounting.[7] Not only has the client often been overpaid, but it is frequently several months before the mistake comes to light. Even if an eagle-eyed cashier spots the error immediately and stops the cheque, think of the effect on your client regardless of whether or not your action is in breach of the guidelines set out in *The Guide to the Professional Conduct of Solicitors 1999*, published by the Law Society. It is the final dealing the client will have with the firm in the transaction and the client's trust and confidence is likely to be wiped out as a result. Firms cannot argue that clients should have realised that they were receiving too much money. It is the firm's responsibility to check completion statements and to have good practice management standards in place to prevent such mistakes. It is up to the partners to ensure that these standards exist and that adequate supervision leads to full compliance. Although the bulk of accounting mistakes occur in conveyancing, other work areas are not exempt.

Confidentiality

Use the induction process to emphasise the importance of confidentiality to all support staff, particularly those who have not worked in the legal profession before. Take a critical look at confidentiality, your office and your reception area in particular. Do not discuss matters with clients there; even just signing documents may be risky. Can other clients overhear your receptionist talking about confidential matters with another client on the phone? Is post left visible? Can clients glimpse information on a computer screen?

CHAPTER SUMMARY

1. Risk management covers all areas of practice management and of work.

2. Establish responsibility for risk management and requisite lines of communication.

3. Promote a culture of openness and of continuous improvement.

4. Client needs should form the basis of systems and procedures.

5. Involve those using systems and procedures in their design.

6. Ensure that appropriate organisational structures exist for supervision and delegation.

7. Take particular care with first meetings.

8. Manage billing to meet clients' expectations.

9. Train fee earners to understand and manage clients' expectations.

Notes

1 J. Verry, 'Ignore risk management at your peril', *Managing Partner*, April 2002 4(10), p.8.
2 Ibid.
3 Solicitors' Indemnity Fund or the Risk Improvement Unit of the Law Society.
4 E. Vere-Jones, 'Gold standard' [2002] *Gazette*, 7 February, 22.
5 'Fox Williams survey' [2002] *Gazette*, 24 January.
6 'Risk management, barriers to implementation', [2002] *Gazette*, 20 June.
7 M. Frith, Office for the Supervision of Solicitors, 'Bin accounting errors and stop complaints' [2001] *Gazette*, 15 April.

14

Handling complaints

KEY POINTS _____

- Firms must understand the difference between a service complaint and a negligence claim
- Firms must have an in-house complaints procedure
- How to handle complaints; be conciliatory
- Learn from your mistakes; why did they occur? How can you prevent them from recurring?

Service complaints and negligence claims: the difference

Many lawyers do not understand the concept of a service complaint.[1]

The divide between the perspectives of solicitor and client is probably at its greatest when it comes to handling complaints. Many solicitors continue to stress the professional and technical aspects of their work and do not acknowledge that legal firms are in business to provide legal services to clients and that to stay in business they must satisfy the needs of those clients. If a client is dissatisfied, the fee earner has not met the client's expectations in respect of the service. We live in a consumerist society and clients are used to having complaints listened to and appropriate recompense given. Unfortunately, the approach of most members of the profession to complaints handling has not improved, probably because the majority still fail to recognise the difference between a complaint about poor service and a claim in respect of technical work. To most solicitors both are a slight on their professional ability and pride and they treat them in the same way – as claims. They do not accept that clients are far more likely to complain about the way in which they have delivered the service rather than their advice itself.

In many ways, firms should welcome complaints. However much we would like to think that we offer a perfect service to our clients, human beings are fallible and there will always be the opportunity for a breakdown in confidence to occur. Firms must endeavour to minimise the occasions on which this happens, but, when it does, they should take whatever steps are necessary to regain the client's confidence and learn from the mistakes that have been made to ensure that they do not happen again. It is far better to know that a client is dissatisfied and to have the opportunity for redress than for the client to moan to his family, friends and colleagues with the consequent damage to the firm's reputation.

Most commercial clients will express their views about service levels. However, few private clients, or owner-managed business clients, complain as readily and most put up with poor service for some time before making a formal complaint. Although only 5 per cent actually make a formal complaint, another 46 per cent complain on a less formal basis, to fee earners, secretaries or a receptionist for example.[2] Clients often say 'I don't want to make a formal complaint but . . .'.

Half of all complaints about delay arise from a lack of communication on the solicitor's part. Clients presume that nothing is happening because they have heard nothing from you. Many complaints begin as a simple misunderstanding and a failure on the fee earner's part to recognise the client's perspective and the client's need for information. The trigger is frequently a failure to return phone calls, not from difficult clients but from those that have a genuine grievance. Clients are not mind-readers – they cannot know what is happening unless you tell them. The next highest number of complaints relates to costs. Fortunately, the number about lack of information on costs at the outset of a matter is falling, indicating that the profession is getting better at providing this information.[3] However, firms still need to improve the levels of ongoing communication and information about costs during a matter.

The requirements of the Solicitors' Costs Information and Client Care Code 1999

The Solicitors' Costs Information and Client Care Code 1999 revised and expanded the requirements of former Practice Rule 15. Section 7(b) of the Code relates to complaints handling and provides that:

(b) Every principal in private practice must:

   i.   ensure the client is told the name of the person in the firm to contact about any problem with the service provided;
   ii. have a written complaints procedure and ensure that all complaints are handled in accordance with it; and
   iii. ensure that the client is given a copy of the complaints procedure on request.

The aim of this section of the Code is that solicitors should be able to deal with any complaints about their service, in-house and in a competent manner. If you handle a complaint without delay and to your client's satisfaction, you stand a far greater chance of retaining the client. The Law Society's Practice Standards Unit publication, *Handling Complaints Effectively* (July 2000) contains precedents for complaints procedures that comply with the Code and that are suitable to give to clients. It is most effective to have one person in the firm to deal with complaints and they are the person to whom all formal complaints should immediately be referred. However, it is also prudent to take heed of the far greater number of 'informal' complaints and to handle these at a departmental level. The same principles apply whatever the level of complaint: the client's dissatisfaction has to be dispelled as quickly as possible.

How to handle a complaint

Your aim should be to retain the client, and complaints are far more likely to be concluded satisfactorily and at much less cost in terms of time, money and stress if they are handled quickly. You are more likely to retain the client's goodwill because if the client's complaint is handled well, it may serve to increase client confidence in the firm. Nip it in the bud by dealing with it comprehensively and in a receptive manner. When a complaint is received, handle it in person and not by correspondence, although you may want to write a short holding letter to let your client know that you are taking immediate steps to look into the complaint and that you will get back to the client very soon. You cannot convey body language or tone in a letter, both of which are essential to resolving issues. Learn to say sorry – that your client has been sufficiently upset to feel he or she has to make a complaint, and that you are extremely sorry that they have been upset, without actually accepting responsibility for their dissatisfaction. Read the file immediately. Discuss it with the relevant fee earner. If it is your own file, pass it to another fee earner for a more objective view. Try to understand the position from your client's perspective, and wherever possible, go to see the client. Inviting clients to your office to discuss the matter will make them feel at a disadvantage because they are on your territory. Do not be aggressive or confrontational, or blame the client, otherwise the problem may spiral out of control. Do not go on the defensive and argue that the client's expectations were totally unreasonable. It was up to you to understand and manage those expectations by informing your client what would be reasonable for them to expect. How might the client have interpreted the way you handled the matter? It is not difficult to pacify a dissatisfied client, provided the complaint is dealt with promptly and sensitively. Make a realistic offer to compensate the client as soon as possible. It will be worth it in terms of the saved time and stress that dealing with a continuing complaint will involve.

Dealing with the complaint may not be straightforward because initially your client may express it in terms of general dissatisfaction with the way in which the client's matter has been handled. It may be hard to identify what lies at the root of it because clients may not be able to articulate exactly what it is they are dissatisfied with. Remember that they are unfamiliar with legal processes and the way in which you run your practice but they know that something is wrong and that the service is not what they had hoped for. By talking to your client, you will gradually understand the source of dissatisfaction. Remember that this may not be the only client who is feeling that way; others may not have told you of their similar dissatisfaction but they will certainly be telling their friends and colleagues.

Sole practitioners are faced with a particularly difficult problem because they have to handle the complaint themselves and may be too close to the situation to understand the client's perspective. If need be, pass the file to another solicitor or to the local law society if it runs a conciliation scheme, so that the matter can be dealt with effectively with minimal time and stress for client and solicitor.

How *not* to handle a complaint

Few solicitors look at a complaint from the client's perspective or accept that there will be two sides to the story and the client may be justified in his or her view. Firms usually deal with the client by letter, which Mike Frith argues is completely the wrong approach.[4] Instead of being conciliatory, the letter will be very formal in tone and probably defensive. The client is unlikely to share the solicitor's letter-writing skills and will choose how to interpret the letter, and may miss your intention completely. Solicitors hold that they are being 'purely professional' when dealing with service complaints. However, the language and tone that this conveys will not be appreciated by a client who wants to hear a response to what he or she considers to be a justifiable complaint. Mike Frith believes that this attitude is understandable because solicitors genuinely believe that they are reacting to a complaint in a professional way. Solicitors exist in an adversarial environment, particularly when it comes to handling claims. Therefore it is natural to act in a similar fashion when a client questions what you have done. In face-to-face meetings, solicitor and client can read each other's body language and the outcome is likely to be far more conciliatory.

The one approach that you should not take is to do nothing. Burying your head in the sand when faced with a complaint will only compound a problem that will not go away.

Learning from your mistakes

Firms frequently waste the opportunity presented by complaints – to learn from them and to improve service as a result. A firm's complaints record contains vital information about how the firm can improve its service. Each claim should be reviewed to see why it arose, what happened, why it happened and what can be done to prevent it happening again. Do not carry out a witch-hunt, but talk to staff to get to the bottom of the problem. It may be time consuming but will be worth it in the long term. Look for any patterns in what happens. Do the complaints centre on one fee earner or department? Are they evidence of a more general attitude within the firm, or endemic to a particular department?

It is important not to overlook the 'informal' complaints as well. The nature of these provides valuable information about ways in which you could improve service levels so that clients understand and appreciate the value of what you actually do for them. A survey of everyone in the firm as to what they think of current client service levels, what they believe the firm has got right and where service could be improved will produce illuminating information. If the firm makes such a survey anonymous, people will feel freer to express their views and you will have an opportunity to pick up on the 'informal complaints', many of which may have been covered up out of loyalty.

Good supervision and an open culture should lead to fee earners feeling able to admit to complaints about their service without being made to feel incompetent or weak. Making a fee earner a scapegoat and sacking him or her is only a short-term solution. You need to get to the root of the problem, which may be grounded in the culture of the firm, in levels of supervision, in the need for training. It is unfair to sack a person if poor management is the cause and your action will be unsettling for remaining staff. Your aim should be to establish how to improve your service to prevent future dissatisfaction. Gather as much information as possible about complaints, learn from it and implement and sustain the requisite changes.

- What systems need to be improved?
- What training do fee earners need?
- Do they need better supervision?
- Are your organisational structures in line with delivering value to your client markets?

CHAPTER SUMMARY

1. Every firm must comply with the Solicitors' Costs Information and Client Care Code 1999.

2. Managers must acknowledge that complaints differ from claims and that they should be handled in a different way. The customer, may after all, be right.

3. Firms should always try to see a claim from the client's perspective and to be conciliatory.

4. Managers should monitor formal and informal complaints, learn from the information and take appropriate action to ensure that the same complaints do not recur.

5. Firms should aim to have an open culture in which mistakes are not viewed as failure but are seen as a learning exercise.

Notes

1   M. Frith, 'Holding the line' [2001] *Gazette*, 7 June.
2   P. Steven (1997) *Keeping Clients: A Client Care Guide for Solicitors*, Law Society Publishing.
3   Ibid.
4   M. Frith, 'Holding the line' [2001] *Gazette*, 7 June.

Further reading

Baker, R. (2001) *The Professional's Guide to Value Pricing*, Harcourt Professional Publishing.

Boutall, T. and Blackburn, B. (2001) *Solicitors' Guide to Good Management: Practical Checklists for the Management of Law Firms*, Law Society Publishing.

Bown-Wilson, D. and Courtney, G. (2002) *Marketing, Management and Motivation*, Law Society Publishing.

Brown, A. (1998) *Organisational Culture*, Pearson Education Limited.

Denney, R., Jordan, C. and Yost, S. (1991) *Keeping Happier Clients: How to Build and Improve Client Relations*, American Bar Association.

Ewalt, H. W. (1994) *Through the Client's Eyes*, American Bar Association.

Freeman, M. (1997) *Client Management for Solicitors*, Cavendish Publishing.

Frith, M. (2001) *The Solicitors' Guide to Complaints Avoidance and Handling*, EMIS Professional Publishing.

Gilligan, C., Lowe, R. and Hedley, A. (2000) *Marketing Legal Services*, CLT Publishing Ltd.

Handy, C. (1995) *The Empty Raincoat*, Random House Business Books.

Hilder, P. (1997) *IT in the Solicitors' Office*, Blackstone Press.

Hussey, D. (2000) CBI Series in Practical Strategy, *Strategy and Planning: A Manager's Guide*, John Wiley & Sons Ltd.

Law Society (2001), *Lexcel Assessment Guide: Practice Management Standards*, Law Society Publishing.

Law Society (1999) *The Guide to the Professional Conduct of Solicitors 1999,* Law Society Publishing.

Moore, M and Dodd, M. (2001), *Lexcel Office Procedures Manual: Practice Management Standards*, Law Society Publishing.

Nelson, N. C. (1996) *Connecting With Your Client: Success Through Improved Client Communication Techniques*, American Bar Association.

Lawrence, P. (2000) *Law on the Internet*, Sweet & Maxwell.

Maister, D. (1997) *Managing the Professional Service Firm*, Touchstone.

Maister, D. (2001) *Practice What You Preach: What Managers Must Do to Create a High Achievement Culture*, Free Press.

Mayson, S. (1997) *Making Sense of Law Firms: Strategy, Structure and Ownership*, Blackstone Press.

Moore, M. (2001) *Quality Management for Law Firms*, Law Society Publishing.

Otterburn, A. (2002) *Profitability and Law Firm Management*, Law Society Publishing.

Paton, J. and McCalman, J. (2000) *Change Management: A Guide to Effective Implementation*, Sage Publications.

Porter, D. (2001) *Business Management for Solicitors*, EMIS Professional Publishing.

Robertson, M.A. and Callaway, J.A. (2002) *Winning Alternatives to the Billable Hour*, 2nd Edition, American Bar Association.

Senge, P., Kleiner, A., Roberts. C., Ross, R., Roth, G. and Smith, B. (1999) *The Dance of Change: The Challenges of Sustaining Momentum in Learning Organisations*, Nicholas Brealey Publishing Ltd.

Sherr, A. (1998) *Client Care for Lawyers*, Sweet & Maxwell.

Silverweig, S. and Allen, R. F. (1976) 'Changing the corporate culture', *Sloan Management Review*, 17(3), pp.33–49.

Walden, J. (1998) *Credit Management for Law Firms*, CLT Publishing Ltd.

Westwood, F. (2000) *Achieving Best Practice: Shaping Professionals for Success*, McGraw-Hill.

Additional resources

Law Society (2001) *Practice Excellence*, series of CD-Roms. (Available from the Law Society Business Centre.)

Practice Standards Unit, *Handling Complaints Effectively*, Law Society. (Available by calling (01527) 883264.)

Index